Walks in the
Wye Valley and
Forest of Dean

Introduction

Copyright Dave Meredith 2020

All rights reserved. No part of this publication may be reproduced, stored in a retrieval system, or transmitted in any form or by any means – electronic, mechanical, photocopying, recording or otherwise – without prior written permission.

Photographs: copyright Dave Meredith 2020

Cover photograph: Bluebells (Walk 20 – Bradley Wood)

Disclaimer: The information in this book is given in good faith and is believed to be correct at the time of publication. Care should always be taken in hill country. Where appropriate, attention has been drawn to matters of safety. The author and publisher cannot take any responsibility for any accidents incurred while following these walks. Only you can judge your own fitness, competence and experience. Do not rely solely on sketch maps for navigation. We strongly recommend the use of appropriate Ordnance Survey (or equivalent) maps.

Walks in the
Wye Valley and
Forest of Dean

Dave Meredith

Introduction

Acknowledgements:

I would like to acknowledge the help given to me by staff at the Cinderford Public Library

Also, many thanks to Ian and Kath Dewar of Ross on Wye who have helped to check the walk directions.

If you would like to contact the author with any suggestions for corrections or improvements please use the e-mail address below:

drgmeredith@gmail.com

Last updated November 2022

Contents

	Introduction		7
1.	Kymin	5½ miles (9km)	15
2.	Whitestone	4½ miles (7km)	22
3.	Tintern	7½ miles (12km)	28
4.	Wyndcliffe	3½ miles (5.5km)	35
5.	Wintours Leap	5 miles (8km)	40
6.	Piercefield	3½ miles (5.5km)	47
7.	Doward	7½ miles (12km)	53
8.	Symonds Yat	5½ miles (9km)	61
9.	Coppet Hill	6½ miles (10.5km)	68
10.	Lydbrook	7 miles (11km)	76
11.	Ruardean Hill	5 miles (8km)	85
12.	Brierley	5½ miles (9km)	93
13.	Speech House	6 miles (9.5km)	101
14.	Darkhill and Bixslade	6 miles (9.5km)	110
15.	Parkend	4 miles (6.5km)	119
16.	Old Park Wood	4 miles (6.5km)	126
17.	Wigpool	6 miles (9.5km)	132
18.	Soudley	6 miles (9.5km)	139
19.	Mallards Pike	5 miles (8km)	148
20.	Bradley Hill Bluebells	4 miles (6.5km)	155
21.	Flaxley	4½ miles (7km)	160
22.	Newent Daffodils	7½ miles (12km)	167

Walks 1 to 6 follow the course of the Wye Tour, popular in Georgian times.

Walks 5 and 6 (Wintour's Leap and Piercefield) may be combined since they have a common start point.

Walks 11 and 12 (Ruardean Hill and Brierley) may be combined since they have a common start point.

Introduction

Dedicated to Fred Wood

Introduction

The Forest of Dean is the greatest tract of native woodland left in Britain. One of our two great forests, it sits on a plateau overlooking two of the longest rivers in these islands – the Wye and the Severn. Its tremendously varied landscape is covered by a myriad of paths and tracks which, combined with the Forestry Commissions' open access policy, make it perfect walking country. Taking you under the dappled shade of its towering oak and beech, and alongside its sylvan Wye, the walks in this book will give you a fascinating glimpse of Dean's rich and diverse history.

The Wye was for many centuries a war zone, marking the boundary of England and Wales, before settling down as an important trade route. Despite its long industrial history of wire-making, iron smelting, copper working and tinplate manufacture, the Wye gorge remains almost completely unspoilt. Having been one of the cradles of the industrial revolution, it can now claim to be the birth-place of tourism.

The Forest of Dean has been shaped by the variety of roles it has served throughout its history: industrial region, royal hunting ground, supplier of timber for the Navy, and more recently a recreational and tourist area. It is an area which has been very much the subject of its own laws, whether they were the harsh royal restrictions imposed in the interests of the deer, or the courts and privileges of the free miners which go back to the 14th century.

For this reason the forest has an insular and secretive feel about it, and from behind its two great rivers it has developed its own dialect and traditions. It enjoys some unique grazing customs under an ancient right bestowed in Norman times which allowed sheep to graze unrestricted through the forest, although in recent times this has become a contentious issue. Few of its towns and villages existed before Victorian times, and many grew in a haphazard fashion around the mines and quarries that provided employment.

Introduction

Local author Winifred Foley described it well: "Ten by twenty miles of secluded, hilly country; ancient woods of oak and fern; and among them small coal mines, small market towns, villages and farms. We are content to be a race apart, made up mostly of families who had lived in the forest for generations".

History

Dean's natural resources have been ruthlessly exploited, to provide timber for the navy, charcoal for the forges, and coal for industrial and domestic use.

The Romans plundered its outcrops of iron ore, leaving the landscape pock-marked with quarries or scowles. The Saxons left behind Offa's dyke, a fortified ditch holding back the troublesome Welsh. William the Conqueror made it a royal forest, a private hunting ground for himself and his successors, with its own code of laws which were administered from St Briavels Castle.

The number of Royal forests declined after the 13th century, when monarchs began to see their commercial possibilities and, as a result, trees were felled, land was sold off, and the forest laws lapsed. As Britain became a maritime nation under the protection of the Royal Navy, the few remaining areas of forest were jealously guarded. Their oaks became an important strategic reserve of shipbuilding timber, and it was said that the commanders of the Spanish Armada were instructed 'to be sure not to leave a single tree standing in the Forest of Dean'. Royal ownership of the forest survived the turmoil of the Civil War, and Charles II created a number of enclosures in order to preserve and re-plant. At the same time Speech House was built, and it soon became the administrative centre of the forest, now managed on behalf of the Crown by the Verderers. They were tasked with resolving the conflicting interests of iron making and mining, with the need to maintain timber stocks for the Navy.

This was often a difficult task because Government policy was not always clear. Originally the Forest had served no other purpose than a royal hunting ground, but leasing the Forest to those who made iron produced a good income for the Treasury. Unfortunately the charcoal needed for iron-making required timber, and this was sometimes taken at the Navy's expense.

The Napoleonic wars severely depleted timber resources and at the request of the Admiralty, large scale plantations were embarked upon. Many of Dean's magnificent stands of mature oak date back to this time and still survive because they became surplus to requirements; the wooden warships of Nelsons time soon being superseded by iron hulled vessels.

The First World War again affected timber resources, and as a consequence the forestry commission was set up in 1919 to repair the damage. The Forest of Dean came under its control a few years later and it began an ambitious programme of conifer planting. In 1938 the Forest of Dean become a National Forest Park and, in a response to an increase in leisure time, the Forestry Commission provided a number of picnic sites and car parks as it strived to balance the needs of tourism and timber conservation.

Mining for iron dates back to Roman times, and many millions of tons of ore were extracted and transported along a network of tramways, which were also used by the coal industry. The free miners were first to exploit the region's coal under rights granted in the 14th century. They tended to work alone or with a partner, and drove their mines into coal seams which existed near the surface, as they continue to do in the few free mines still working today. The Industrial Revolution brought much greater demand for coal, and some free miners leased their rights to outside investors who had the capital and expertise required to reach the deeper and larger reserves of coal. This was then mined on an industrial scale, and the old tramways were upgraded or replaced by railways. As the 20th century wore on, most of the economic reserves of deep-mined coal and iron became exhausted, resulting in the gradual closure of mines and railways. Although the last of the big pits closed in 1965, the tradition of free mining still exists – but only just!

Introduction

Not since medieval times has the Forest been as quiet or as peaceful. Most of its' industrial landscape has been reclaimed by nature, which has restored Dean to a level of beauty and majesty not seen in generations.

The Walks

The Forest of Dean and Wye Valley is a paradise for both the keen rambler and the casual stroller. There are hundreds of miles of easy footpaths taking you to spectacular viewpoints, along woodland glades carpeted with bluebells, daffodils and foxgloves, and under the dappled shade of its golden autumn canopy.

Unfortunately, the forest is a plateau riven by countless streams and rivers, which mean that inevitably there will be some muddy sections and lengthy climbs. Not surprisingly, a dramatic view usually implies a matching level of effort!

Fields. Who likes them? How many of us enjoy tramping round the muddy margins of a maize field accumulating great clods of earth?

Fields have been kept to a minimum – most walks have none at all. Routes have been chosen to make way-finding as easy as possible, but this will inevitably depend on the time of year, a path easy to follow in May can be a metre high with ferns and bramble just a couple of months later.

Obstruction however, is another issue. If you encounter an access problem and you are sure you are on a public right of way, then few landowners would object to you making a detour to get round the problem (although strictly speaking you would then be trespassing!). On returning home, the obstruction should be reported to the Rights of Way Officer of the relevant County Council in order for the issue to be resolved. Nowadays this can be done on-line. Remember that much of the area is a working forest, so, although the details were correct at the time of writing, you may find that trees have been felled and tracks widened.

All walks use public rights of way or pass through areas governed by the Forestry Commission, who have declared their land as 'open access' under the terms of the Countryside & Rights of Way Act 2000 (commonly referred to as 'the right to roam'). This act does not entitle you to walk wherever you like; its benefits applying only within defined areas of open countryside such as mountain, moor, heath land, down land and registered common land. These areas are indicated on the latest copies of the O.S. range of maps, and give you the chance to legally wander away from the beaten track for the first time.

Walks in this book are all contained within the area covered by Ordnance Survey Explorer Map OL14, and even the OS Landranger 162 map covers them all with the exception of walk 22 (Newent). A suitable OS map should be used to supplement the one given in the text which is not to scale, having been drawn to exaggerate the paths and features found along the route.

A grid reference is given for the starting point of each walk. The first three digits are 'eastings' and correspond to the numbers along the bottom edge of the map, while the second three are 'northings', corresponding to the numbers along the map's vertical edge.

--------------------<{}>--------------------
Never judge a queue by its length

Introduction

The Countryside Code

Enjoy the countryside and respect its life and work

Guard against all risk of fire

Keep dogs under close control

Leave gates and property as you find them

Keep to public paths across farmland

Use gates and stiles to cross fences, hedges and walls

Leave livestock, crops and machinery alone

Help to keep all water clean

Protect plants and animals, and take your litter home

Take special care on country roads

Make no unnecessary noise – consider other people

Be safe – plan ahead and follow any signs

Wild Boar

Wild Boar were illegally introduced into the Forest of Dean in 2004. Their presence is controversial.

Wild boar are normally secretive, and largely nocturnal if left alone. They are unlikely to attack people. There have, however, been a number of problems with Boar in the Forest of Dean with damage or injury to people, pets and property. You are unlikely to encounter one but churned up grass verges and disturbed topsoil are evidence of their presence.

What should I do to avoid problems with wild boar?
Do not feed the boar - feeding encourages them into closer contact with humans where the scope for less desirable activity increases

The vast majority of incidents occur when there is a dog present so keep your dog under close control. A number of dogs have been seriously injured by the boar and it is best to avoid this interaction if at all possible. It would be advisable to keep your dog on a lead between February and May when newly born Boar may be encountered.

Do not walk through dense undergrowth where wild boar may be encountered at close quarters.

What should I do if I encounter a wild boar?
Do not approach them – if possible leave the area by the same route you approached by, or make a detour giving the animals a wide berth.

If you have a dog off its lead, call the dog to heel and put the lead on it immediately.

If your dog chases a boar, stay at a safe distance and continue to call the dog back – do not approach the boar or interfere.

Introduction

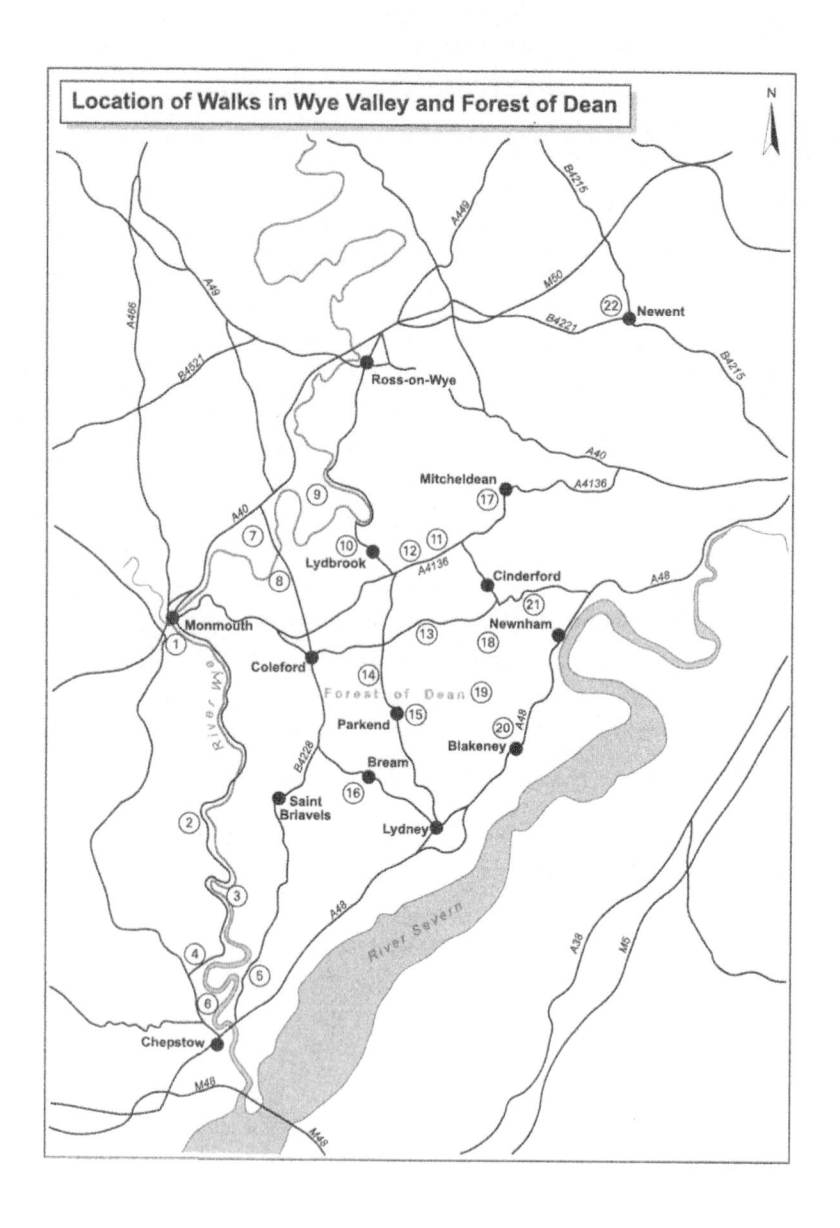

Walk1: The Kymin

The first tourists

A hilly walk with one or two strenuous climbs, but your effort will be amply rewarded with views from almost every part of the route. Even the woodland sections have something to offer with magnificent stands of mature oak and beech. Directions will have to be carefully followed at times but paths are good throughout.

Distance	5½ miles (9 km)
Route	Staunton – Kymin – Buckstone
Maps	OS Explorer Map OL14, and OS Landranger 162
Getting there	The walk starts from Staunton on the A4136 a few miles west of Monmouth
Start/Parking	Park in Staunton next to the church on the north side of the A4136. A track leaves the road on the Monmouth side of the churchyard wall, where a car can be left on the verge. Be careful not to block access to the churchyard
OS Grid Ref/Postcode	SO535942 / GL16 8NU

The Wye Tour

The beauty of the Wye valley was 'discovered' late in the 18th century. Locked in a war with France that would last two decades, the British gentry were forced to have what we might today call a 'holiday at home'.

In 1745 a rector from Ross was the first to build a boat especially to take his guests on excursions down the Wye. By the end of the century there were at least eight boats operating commercially in response to a demand created by a book published in 1783 by artist and vicar William Gilpin. The book was titled *'Observations on the River Wye, and Several Parts of South Wales'* and was the first of several such books Gilpin published covering various British destinations. Illustrated using the new 'aquatint' process, these books can claim to be the first modern guidebooks, and with them their author 'created' tourism. For Gilpin, both texture and composition were important and in his book he expounded his 'principles of picturesque beauty'. Wordsworth, Turner and Coleridge did the tour, no doubt clutching Gilpin's leather bound book, and left inspiring records of their own trips in paintings, poetry and prose.

Boats were hired from inns in Ross and Monmouth, the owner providing a crew of three, one to steer and two to row. Food and wine were also to be enjoyed on the trip, which generally took two days going downstream with a mid-way stop at Monmouth. Tourists dined at particular locations, walked up to viewpoints, and visited specific romantic ruins. With the popularity of the tour, it became fashionable to build summerhouses at sites with spectacular viewpoints.

The period 1770 to 1830 was the heyday of the Tour, which became over-commercialised and much less leisurely in the later nineteenth century. However, the beauty of the Wye Valley remains undimmed from Gilpin's days, when its craggy lookouts – Eagle's Nest, Devil's Pulpit and Lover's Leap – were named by these first 'tourists'.

The river was also an important trade route, especially before the arrival of the canals and railways. Prior to the construction of the tow path in 1811, flat bottomed barges were man-hauled as far as Hereford by 32 men harnessed eight at a time in relays. It was desperately hard work – each man hauling a ton of cargo. No doubt the 'society' ladies on their tour boat, fanning themselves in the sultry summer heat, were found looking the other way!

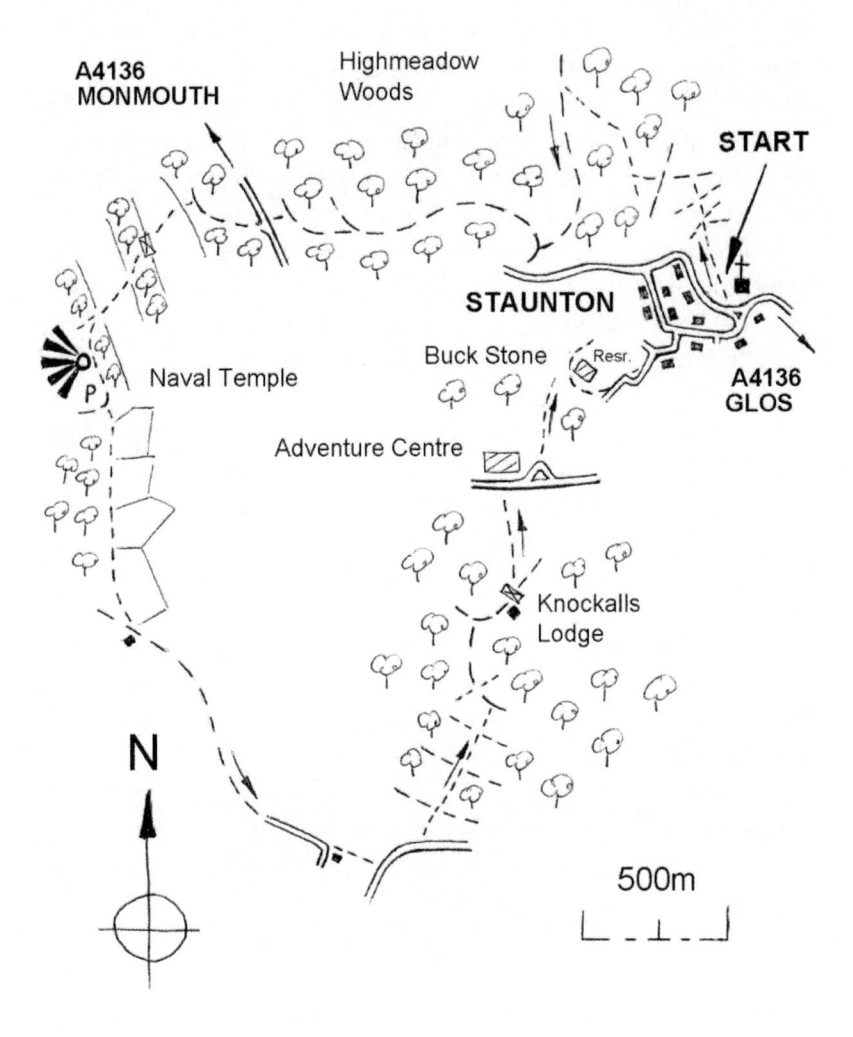

Walks in the Wye Valley and Forest of Dean

The Kymin

This walk takes in one of the surviving summer houses with its 'picturesque' view.

The walk

Walk away from the main road along a metalled track. This ends after about 200m, after which you take a path that passes to the left of a conifer to head straight on into the woodland. Follow the path for about 150m, until a junction of four paths is reached. Take the furthest left of the three paths which head off into the woodland in front of you, ignoring the path over your left shoulder which crosses a stile. Follow this path down through the woodland, with its heady aroma of wild garlic, until a T-junction is reached. Turn left here, and climb up to a forestry road, which you cross to pick up the path again on the other side.

This path drops down to another, where you turn right to find yourself walking alongside a fence. Follow the fence when it turns left and drop down to a forestry track. Turn left here to follow the track through the trees until finally, another track sweeps across in front of you. Turn right here and walk gently downhill, under the shade of some towering oak and beech, until a fork is reached. Turn left here, ignoring the other track which falls away to the right. After about 300m, a path climbs away to the left near a Wysis way-mark post. Follow this up to the road where you turn left, and then right, onto a track which climbs away from the other side of the road. Follow this track through some magnificent old woodland until a field becomes visible through the trees to the left. Take a path which leaves the track here, and pass through a gate to enter the field.

Bear slightly right here, and climb up the field heading for the middle of the tree line on the far side. About half way up, a gate becomes visible under the shade of an oak tree. Pass through this gate and follow this path up through the trees to another field. As you approach the field, use the fence on your left as a guide, and head out across this field aiming for a point where the deciduous trees end and the conifers begin. On the other side of this field, go through a kissing gate and fork left to reach the Kymin Roundhouse.

Today's Tourists

With the popularity of the 'Wye tour', it became fashionable to build summerhouses at sites with spectacular viewpoints, and this is one such place. With one of the best views around, this small two-storey circular Georgian banqueting house was built in 1794 by the Monmouth Picnic Club. It played an important part in the local gentry's social calendar with the gentlemen of Monmouth meeting here on Tuesdays for open air lunch parties. Monmouth is spread out before you and a display board lists the hills that can be seen along the horizon.
Just beyond the Roundhouse a short path leads to the Naval Temple, which was built in 1801 as a monument to several British admirals, including Nelson, who a few years earlier celebrated his victory at the Battle of the Nile. Nelson took the tour in 1802, no doubt clutching his copy of Gilpin's guide book and, as word got around that the 'Hero of the Nile' was in the area, his holiday

swiftly turned into a triumphal procession along a riverbank lined by cheering spectators. As his boat from Ross came into view, some four-pounder guns here sounded a salute to greet him, and when his boat approached Monmouth for his overnight stop, the townsfolk insisted on pulling in his boat, breaking out in a chorus of "Hail the Conquering Hero". On a subsequent visit he enjoyed breakfast in the nearby Roundhouse and thought the view was one of the finest in the country, but left the area concerned about the state of Navy timber in the forest.

Follow the gravel drive to the left of the Naval Temple until it reaches the car park. Just beyond this, as the drive bears right, go through a kissing gate next to a pair of wrought iron driveway gates on the left. Follow this path, which hugs a boundary fence, until you reach another kissing gate, after which the path passes through the first of four fields. At the end of the fourth, pass through a gate near a cottage and turn left to follow a track, which continues downhill for almost 1000m, until becoming a metalled lane near a farm. Go straight on down the lane for about 150m, until it bends right in front of a cottage. Leave the road here, taking a path off to the left, which eventually passes behind the cottage, and follow this path which drops steeply down into Redbrook. At the bottom, turn left onto the road and follow it for about 100m around a right hand bend, until another path climbs away from the road near a telegraph pole on the left. Keep on the left hand side of the road as your visibility of on-coming traffic is limited here.

Walk up this overgrown path as it climbs steeply away from the road, until it enters the woodland, where you begin the long steady climb up to the Buck Stone. Follow the path up and, after crossing two forestry tracks and a footpath, you climb up to a rarely used forestry track. Turn left here and, after about 250m, turn right and walk up to a gate beside Knockalls Lodge. Just beyond the Lodge's driveway, take a left turn onto a path which soon follows a fence up through the woodland. Eventually, you leave the fence behind, and walk up through an open area of scrubland before the trees close in again as you approach the Buckstone Adventure Centre. Keep left at a fork in the path before arriving at the access road to the centre. Turn right onto this and, at the end of the buildings, turn left onto a track that climbs away from the road. This soon bends right but you continue on to follow an indistinct path which heads straight on into the woodland about 20 metres to the right of a power line. Shortly, a wall appears on the left, and you follow this until a gate allows you through the wall to the Buck Stone and its wonderful view towards the Black Mountains. The Buckstone used to rock before it was dislodged in 1885.

Walk back to the gate, and walk a few metres beyond it to turn right onto a track, which skirts the right hand side of Staunton Reservoir. This soon bends left to reach a lane where Newland Church is visible away to the right. Turn left onto this lane, and follow it until a you reach a sharp right hand bend, where you continue straight on using a path which leaves the outside of the bend. This soon drops onto another lane where you turn left near a cottage. Walk down a steep hill to reach a road junction near a power line and turn right, following the lane round to the left to enter the village of Staunton. Turn right at the next junction onto a road that was the main thoroughfare through the village until the turnpike road (now the A4136) was built in 1831. Follow the road to the left of an old animal pound until you climb up to the start of the walk near the church of All Saints, which dates back to the 12th Century. In the churchyard can be seen the grave of David Mushet who, with his son, helped to revolutionise the steel industry (see walk 14).

--------------------<{}>--------------------
Whoever is happy will make others happy too

Walk2: Whitestones
A whiff of scandal!

A delightful walk mostly along woodland tracks and old country lanes, with some memorable views of the Wye Valley. One gentle climb but paths are good throughout.

Distance	4½ miles (7 km)
Route	Whitestone – Cleddon – Catbrook
Maps	OS Explorer Map OL14, and OS Landranger 162
Getting there	The walk starts from the Whitestones Car park just south of Llandogo on the A466
Start/Parking	From Llandogo, take the turning next to the shop (signposted Trellech) Follow the road for about 1½ miles until, just after a long right hand bend, the car park can be seen on the right next to a road junction.
OS Grid Ref/Postcode	SO523029 / NP16 6NF

The walk

Walk away from the road, following the tarmac as it climbs to the right. Continue uphill to reach a picnic site where you bear left, looking for a track beyond a forestry barrier. Round the barrier and make a gentle climb up through stately oaks and beech trees, keeping the valley on your right.

It is thought that the views ahead inspired William Wordsworth to write 'Lines composed a few miles above Tintern Abbey' when he visited the area for the second time in 1798. The three viewpoints along this track are each provided with a bench from which to admire the changing view.

After the third viewpoint, follow the track round to the left shortly arriving at a T-junction where you turn right. Follow the path as it narrows through the trees until it joins a walled track which arrives from the left. Go straight on here until, after passing to the left of a small pasture, you arrive a junction of paths. Take the path ahead of you, ignoring the path on the left and the track on the right. After walking along another section of walled track you arrive at a bend in a narrow road. Here you turn left to follow the lane between two cottages. Before you do this, look for a path on the right which drops down a few steps to Cleddon Falls – well worth a visit after a period of heavy rain.

After passing between the cottages, look out for a left turn after about 100 metres. This is your route, but before you walk down this short cul-de-sac, continue along the lane for about 200 metres until you reach a country house standing at the end of an avenue of trees on the right. This is Cleddon Hall – in Victorian times the childhood home of Nobel prize-winning philosopher Bertrand Russell.

Bertrand's rather unconventional parents, Lord and Lady Amberley, were both advocates of radical causes. They were ostracized by polite society because of their vocal support for women's suffrage, equal pay for women, and birth control. Their unusual behaviour extended into the family home, where Lady Amberley had a sexual relationship with Douglas Spalding, the children's tutor, who suffered with tuberculosis.

Whitestones

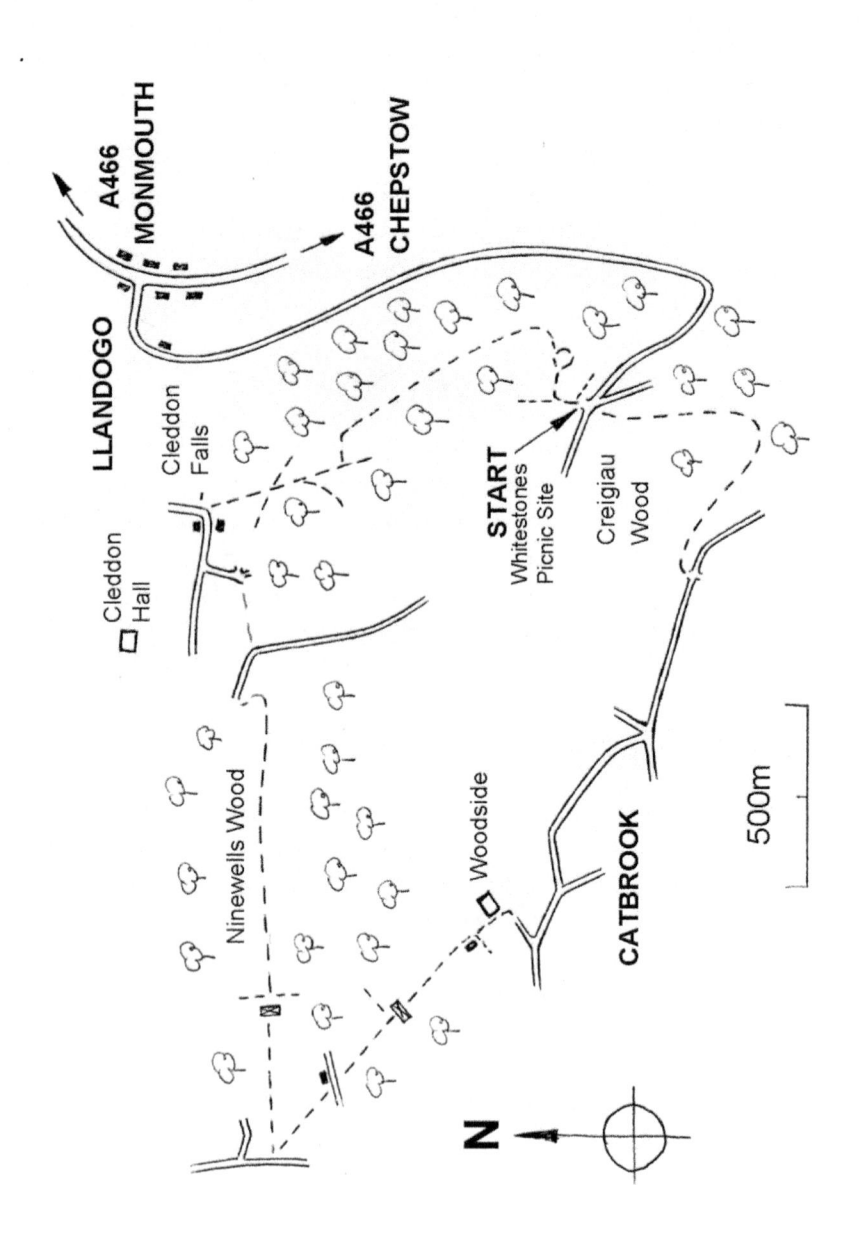

The Amberleys took the view that while Spalding ought to remain childless, due to his condition, it was unfair to expect him to remain celibate, so Lady Amberly slept with him on occasions!

Despite their eccentricities, the Amberleys were by all accounts fun loving people, and life at Cleddon for the first year of Bertrand's life was quiet and even idyllic. However, tragedy struck the infant Russell when his mother and sister died of Diptheria. His father died shortly afterwards leaving the boy in the care of his grandmother.
He was educated at home by a series of tutors and Russell was to describe his childhood as bleak and lonely. Only his wish to know more about mathematics kept him from suicide. When Russell was eleven years old, his brother Frank introduced him to the work of Euclid, which he described in his autobiography as "one of the great events of my life, as dazzling as first love".

Unsurprisingly in the face of such tragedy, there are paranormal tales -the ghost of Lady Amberley is rumoured to ride the forest paths on horseback.

Return to the cul-de-sac mentioned earlier where, after walking to the right of a white-washed cottage, you reach the end of the road. Ignore the driveway and the farm gates and instead, walk into the far right-hand corner to find an un-gated bridleway, one of many used by the Amberleys to visit friends in their pony and trap. After a while the path passes to the right of a substantial cottage before climbing up to a road.

Turn right here and walk about 200m until a forestry track (Ninewells Wood) appears on the left. Turn onto this track and follow it past the car park. Continue with it as it climbs a long right-hand bend before straightening out.
Stay on this long straight track for about 800m, ignoring a number of minor paths that lead off to the left and right, until the track narrows to a path before reaching a stile in a fence. Cross the stile

and walk into a dense plantation of young oak trees, all straining to reach the sunlight.

Whitestones Viewpoint

Eventually another stile is crossed, and soon afterwards a stone stile is reached leading to a road. Don't cross this stile but look over your left shoulder for another path that leads back into the woodland. Follow this path through the trees, eventually crossing another stile, to reach a narrow lane near a bungalow. Look slightly left across the lane to find a wooden five-bar gate and follow the path beyond it through the woodland. Carry straight on at the next gate you encounter, ignoring a path that leads away to the left

Soon the woodland gives way to pasture land and, after passing to the left of a cottage, you proceed straight on through a gate, ignoring the farm gate on the right. Continue through the trees to arrive at Woodside – a busy riding stable.

Next to the stables, turn right onto a driveway which leads down to a road. Turn left when you reach the road and further on, as you reach the small village of Catbrook, fork left onto a minor road which passes a number of well-tended cottages and gardens.

Eventually you drop down to a T-junction, where you turn left to follow the road down and away from the village. After a while, the road enters some woodland and, just before it bends to the right, you find a way-mark post on the left opposite a forestry track. Leave the road here and follow the path which runs parallel to the road for a short distance before eventually leaving it behind. The path is shaded by some towering oak trees as it passes through Creigau Wood to reach the start of the walk about 800m away. If you are leading the walk you can confidently tuck this book under your arm and impress your fellow walkers by smugly announcing that you know your way back from here!

--------------------<{}>--------------------

I spoke to somebody at Wonga
'Cause I wasn't financially stronga
I borrowed with lust
The company went bust
So now I'm in debt no longa

Walk3: Tintern

An ancient frontier

A walk that has everything: A viewpoint, a number of historical sites, a riverside walk, some delightful woodland – even an animal hospital! The route follows an old railway line away from the village before climbing up the side of the Wye valley to reach a renowned viewpoint. From here you trace the path of an ancient frontier through deciduous woodland before returning via a riverside path. One long strenuous climb but paths are good throughout.

Distance	7½ miles (12km)
Route	Tintern – Devil's Pulpit – Brockweir
Maps	OS Explorer Map OL14, and OS Landranger 162
Getting there	The walk start from the centre of Tintern which lies on the A466 Chepstow-Monmouth road.
Start/Parking	South of Tintern Garage there are a few stretches of roadside parking between the road and the river. Failing this there is an ample car park near the abbey
OS Grid Ref/Postcode	SO528005 / NP16 6SE

Tintern

Tintern is famous for its Abbey, which was founded in 1131 during the reign of King Henry I. It was home to around four hundred monks, and its land, divided into agricultural units or granges, provided employment for many local people. For 400 years it dominated the economy of the surrounding area until it was destroyed in 1536 as part of the Dissolution of the Monasteries.

Industrial activity began soon after, when a wire-works was established producing wire for a wide variety of industries. The site was convenient, because the Wye offered transportation, the local stream provided power, trees in the nearby woodland could be used to make charcoal, and a ready supply of minerals and ore were available locally. For 300 years, the numerous works and forges near Tintern dominated the village and surrounding communities. By the late 18th century Tintern had become the climax of the 'Wye Tour' (see walk 1) and with completion of the new turnpike road (now the A466) in 1828, and the arrival of the Wye Valley Railway in the 1870s, visitor numbers greatly increased. As a result, tourism became the mainstay of Tintern's economy and remains so today.

The walk

Head towards the steel girder bridge which crosses the river in the centre of the village next to the Abbey Mill.

When the Wye Valley Railway Line was constructed in 1876, it bypassed Tintern on the other side of the river, much to the indignation of the owners of the wireworks who demanded a connection across the river. The resulting branch line and bridge was built at great cost by the Railway Company to placate the local industrialists, but even before completion, the wire-works had ceased trading and as a consequence, the bridge became largely redundant.

After crossing the bridge bear right, and follow the obvious path which climbs gently away from the river. Ignore a path which climbs away to the left, and press on for another 300m until you

Tintern

pass to the right of a railway tunnel. This was the point where the branch line joined the Wye Valley Railway. Ignore this and follow the old track-bed through the woodland for well over 1500m.

You can now relax for a while but start paying attention again when the line begins a long slow left-hand bend in a shallow cutting. Once out of the cutting you reach a fork in the track (ignore a path which drops down to the river on the right). Take the left fork and climb away from the old trackbed (which continues on to the newly opened Tiddenham Tunnel).

View from Devil's Pulpit

Walks in the Wye Valley and Forest of Dean

BROCKWIER

TINTERN

Station

Lippets Grove

Devils Pulpit

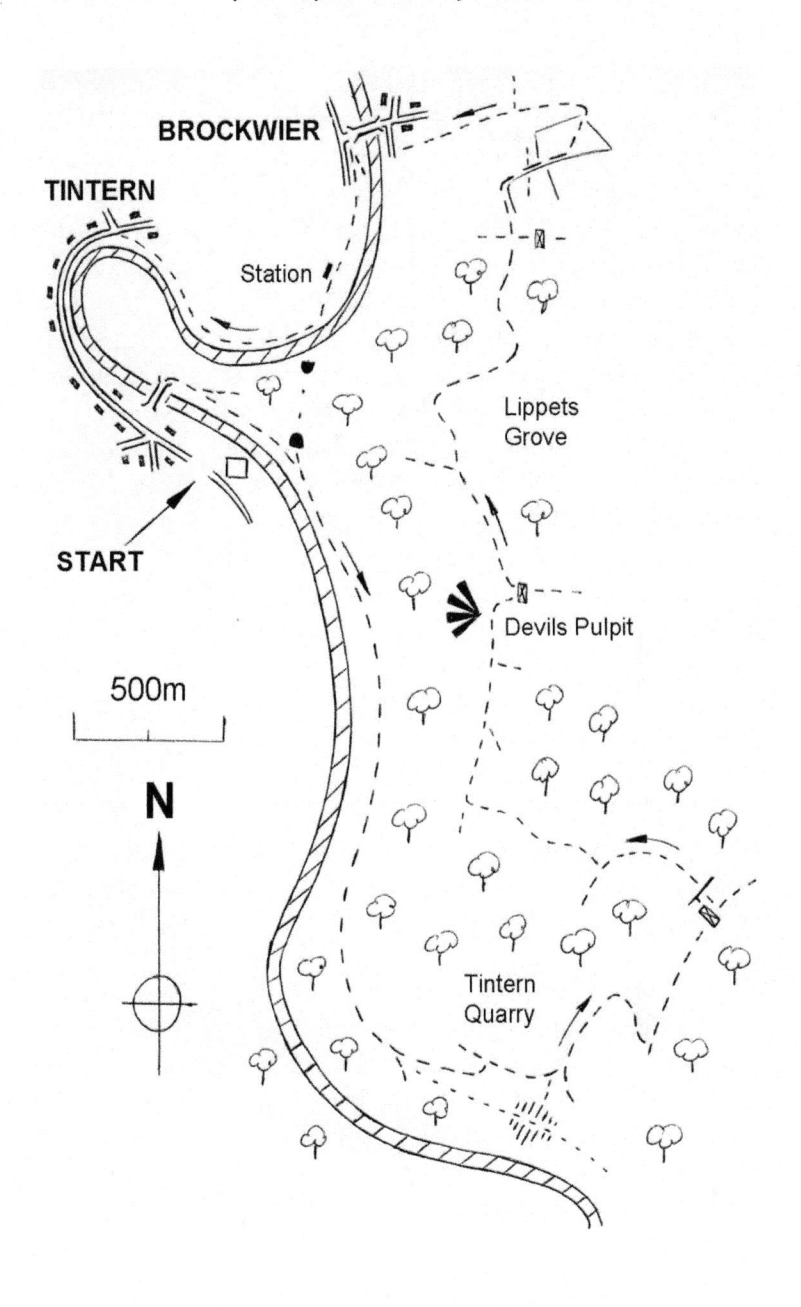

START

500m

N

Tintern Quarry

Tintern

After about 100m, the track reaches a T-junction. Turn right here and follow a level path for a distance before dropping down into a narrow valley. At the bottom, ignore a faint path which drops away to the right and press on for a few metres to reach a broad gravelly track. Turn left here and begin a steep climb uphill. After a while the track bends round to the right, finally levelling off on a ledge with open views across the woodland. Walk beyond this to reach another track where you turn left. You now resume your steady climb until you eventually reach a metal gate. Walk round the gate and, ignoring the track ahead of you, look to the left for a forestry barrier and take the track beyond it into the trees. You are now on the Offa's Dyke footpath, a well sign-posted route which you follow all the way to Brockweir, about 4 km away.

Follow the broad track as it undulates through the woodland for over 600m until a footpath appears on the right by a way-mark post. Turn right here, and follow the obvious path for about 1km until, after passing close by a field, it becomes edged with stone on the approach to the Devil's pulpit.

You are now following the line of Offa's Dyke, a fortified earthwork built by the powerful Anglo-Saxon King of Mercia in the second half of the 8th century in order to establish a frontier between his kingdom and the troublesome Welsh.

Soon a clearing heralds your arrival at the magnificent viewpoint of the Devil's Pulpit. From here the view of the Abbey is dramatically framed by the surrounding beech trees and this rocky vantage point was, according to legend, the rostrum from which Satan canvassed the monks below to join the opposition.

Follow the path away from the viewpoint until you reach a junction of paths near a way-mark post. Off to the right, through a kissing gate, is a path to Tidenham Car Park, but you turn left here to continue along the Offas' Dyke path which is signposted to Brockweir. Follow the path through tall stands of beech trees to another way-mark post, where a path drops down to the left to

Tintern. Ignore this, and press on for some distance until, at the bottom of a hill, the path is eventually crossed by another which passes through a farm gate to reach a field on the right. Continue straight on here and follow the path down through the trees until you reach the corner of a field where you turn right. Continue alongside the fence for as long as you can until, just before the end of the second field, another path drops left near a way-mark post. Turn left here to follow the path down into a field where, by heading slightly right, you reach a stile in the bottom right hand corner. Cross the stile and continue downhill following the path as it swings left near a way-mark post. Keep to the left of the field all the way down to Gregory Farm, an equine welfare centre. Follow the gravel track to the left of this until you reach a road. Turn right here and walk into Brockweir.

Brockweir was an important boat building centre and river port before the arrival of the turnpike road. The larger river boats, flat-bottomed barges known as trows, sailed upstream from Chepstow as far as Brockweir where their cargoes were unloaded onto smaller boats for transport further up river.

Turn left at the road junction near the Brockweir Inn and cross the river using the road bridge. Before you reach the road junction on the far side, look out for a path that drops down some steps on the left. At the bottom, go straight on in the direction of Tintern Station, which is reached along the former track-bed of the Wye Valley Railway; often described as the most beautiful railway journey in Britain.

Tintern was the busiest station on the line, and the duties of the staff at this charming rural station were many and varied. They would typically include lighting the oil lamps, maintaining the station garden, and the collection and delivery of light parcels. The station was not connected to the mains water supply so one thankless task was to fill the tank that supplied the toilet cisterns. This was filled twice a day using a hand pump linked to a nearby well, while drinking water was sent up the line from Chepstow in a milk churn. In the 1950's it was possible to spend a week's holiday at the station in a camping coach (a specially converted old coach) parked in a siding. One holiday maker recalled the stationmaster stopping the train short of the platform so she could have a quantity of hot water from the engine for nappy washing! Let's hope things have improved since then! The most popular trains were the special excursions laid on to Tintern Abbey on the night of the harvest moon. Each September over 1000 people would arrive by train from all over the south west to see the moon shining through the Abbey's Rose window. When the Wye Valley line was constructed, the industries it was intended to serve were already in decline, and much of the increasing tourist traffic that could have remedied the situation was being lost to road transport. When the line closed in 1964, the station escaped the inevitable destruction that normally accompanies closure thanks to the efforts of Gwent County Council and the Countryside Commission who turned the station into a picnic site and visitor attraction.

Walk through the station, following the narrow gauge railway on your left, until you reach a turntable and viewpoint at the far end. Turn right here and follow some steps down to the riverbank where another right turn takes you through a gate and on to a riverside path, which is followed all the way back to Tintern. Eventually the path crosses the left-hand side of a church yard, and after leaving it by a wrought iron gate, you reach a narrow back-street. Bear slightly right here and walk up to the main road where you turn left. Follow the road back to the start.

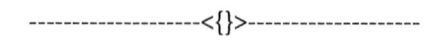

--------------------<{}>--------------------
The beauty of not planning is that failure comes as a complete surprise and is not preceded by a period of doubt and worry

Walk4: Wyndcliffe
–Georgian graffiti

Although you begin this spectacular walk with a steep climb, you are rewarded with a visit to two of the Wye's most romantic viewpoints; 'Eagles Nest' and 'Lovers Leap'. These two airy locations were popularised by the 'Wye Tours' of the late 18th and early 19th centuries (see walk 1). There are one or two exposed sections so please bear this in mind if you have children with you.

Distance	3½ miles (5.5km)
Route	Lower Wyndcliffe – Porthcasseg – Piercefield Cliff
Maps	OS Explorer Map OL14, and OS Landranger 162
Getting there	The walk starts from the Lower Wyndcliffe Carpark which lies 2½ miles north of Chepstow on the A466
Start/Parking	The Lower Wyndcliffe Carpark. The main road twists and turns in this area so care will be needed to spot this secluded car park on the south side of the A466
OS Grid Ref/Postcode	SO527972 / NP16 6HD

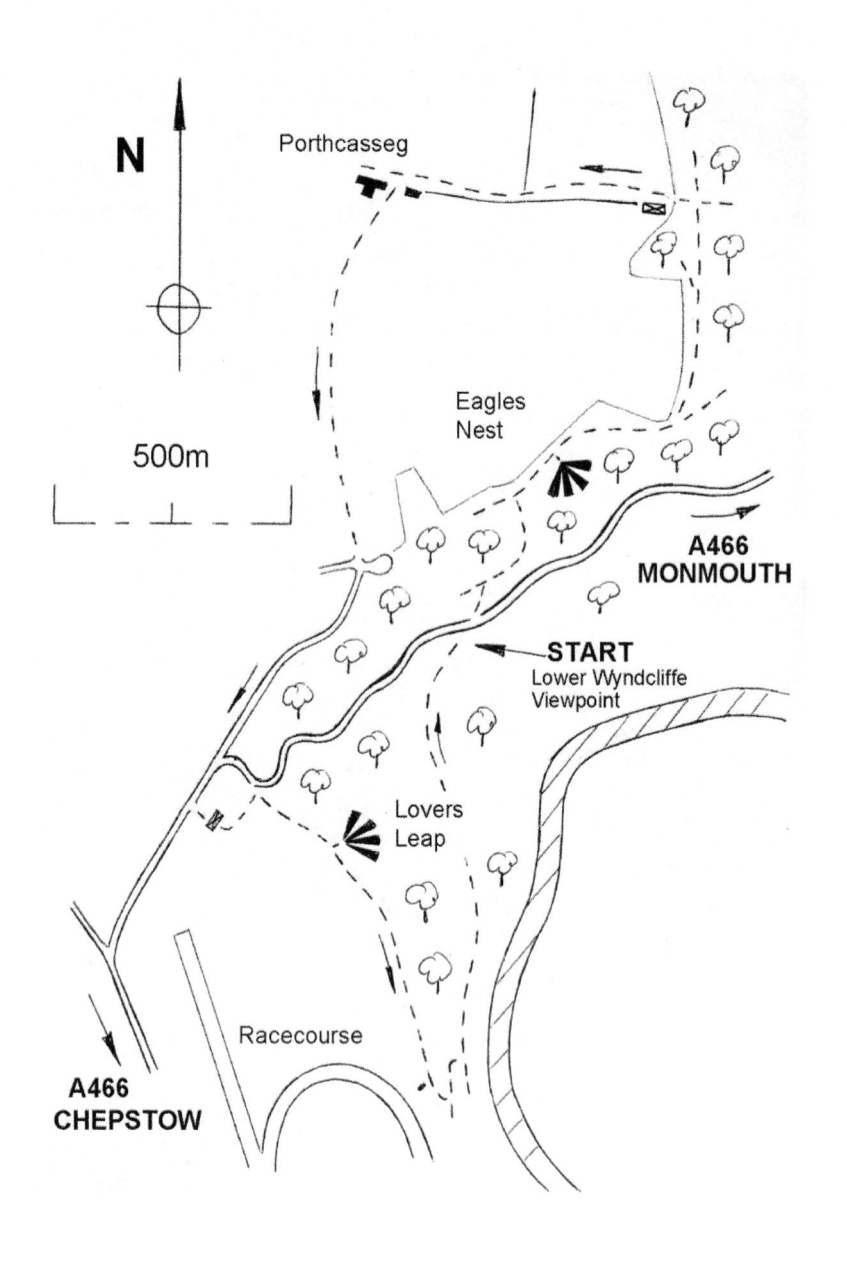

Wyndcliffe

The Walk

Carefully cross the busy A466 and head into the woodland following a way-marked path – 'The Eagles Trail' (or more ominously -the '365 steps') which was built by the Duke of Beaufort in 1828. This rises to a 'T' junction where you bear right after which the ascent begins in earnest. The path begins to climb steeply up through gnarled tree roots and moss-covered boulders until it appears to be blocked by the battlements and towers of Wyndcliffe. Suddenly its walls are breached by a steel staircase which leaps across the only gap in its defences. (Note that the steps can be slippery in wet weather so please use the handrail provided)

At the top it begins to level out, and soon you reach a junction of paths where you turn right. Follow the path through the woodland for about 100m, until another path heads off to the right. Your route is straight on here, but turn right onto this path and walk the short distance down to 'Eagles Nest', a commanding viewpoint over the Wye Gorge and the more distant Severn Estuary.

It's easy to see why the gentry, denied their foreign holidays by Napoleons continental adventures, were so enamoured by this view as they made their tours down the Wye Gorge (see walk 1). In the stone seats at the viewpoint can be seen the engraved names of some of these early 'tourists' who, no doubt, engaged the services of a local stone mason in order to leave their names for posterity.

Return to the point mentioned earlier, and now turn right, following the path which keeps close to the boundary of a field. Eventually a path tempts you down to the right but press on with the field clearly visible on the left. Soon the field is left behind, and after ignoring a faint path forking left you press on for another 120m until you reach a junction of paths where a stile can be seen on the left. Cross this stile and enter the field. Ignore the gate on your left and walk straight on, keeping to the right of a hedgerow.

Wyndcliffe

Pass into a second field using a stile, eventually arriving at the outskirts of Porthcasseg Farm. Keep to the right of its two barns, before turning left to follow an obvious track between the barns and the farm buildings themselves.

Leave the farm behind and, after passing through two gates, the track crosses an open pasture. Half way across this field, an old lime kiln can be seen on your left near a disused quarry. Exit the field at the bottom and continue a short distance to a sharp bend in a road. To the left is the car park for the Upper Wyncliffe viewpoint, but you must continue straight on down the road, which eventually makes a junction with the A466. Go straight ahead here and keep to the right- hand side of the busy road until a pavement appears after a few metres. Walk along this, and look out for the second of two driveways that leave the road on the left. Cross the road and walk down this second driveway where, ahead of you, is a stile and gate in a boundary wall. Pass through the stile, and turn left to walk up the left hand side of a field. In its corner is another stile which takes you into woodland. As the path swings to the right, it passes an ornamental wall on the left where traffic on the busy A466 can be seen a few metres away through a gap. Ignore this and continue to the right through the woodland. The Wye gorge can be glimpsed through the trees on the left and soon your curiosity is satisfied by a short path to the left leading to Lovers Leap. Return to the path where you now turn left to continue in the direction you were heading.

Eventually the railings of Chepstow Racecourse can be glimpsed through the trees, and soon a path leads off towards it on the right. Ignore this, and continue down a few steps to turn left at a junction of paths. This zig-zags down a few metres to a second junction where once again you turn left.

This path now returns you directly to the car-park just over 800m away. No further directions are needed, so put this book away and enjoy the walk along the path, now perched on a leafy ledge high above the river. Your route appears to be obstructed by a limestone bluff at one point but you should find a way through somehow!

Lover's Leap

Walk 5: Wintours Leap
–A desperate ploy

Some agility and stout footwear will be needed on this walk which visits a spectacular viewpoint before returning under the towering cliffs of the Wye gorge. Careful route finding will be needed to negotiate an exposed rock-fall but paths are good throughout. There are one or two exposed sections which make this walk unsuitable for children. Not for the faint-hearted!

Distance	5 miles (8 km)
Route	Tutshill – Lancaut
Maps	OS Explorer Map OL14, and OS Landranger 162
Getting there	The walk starts from the Castle Dell Car Park in Chepstow
Start/Parking	The Castle Dell car park is next to the north east corner of Chepstow Castle. From outside the town, follow the signs to the town centre, and then to the castle itself
OS Grid Ref/Postcode	ST535942 / NP16 5GA

The Walk

Turn left on leaving the car park and walk along Bridge Street with Chepstow Museum on your right. Continue ahead at the junction with St Anne Street, and cross the Wye using the cast iron road bridge built in 1816.

The Wye and Severn share the distinction of having the second highest tidal range in the world, and this is best appreciated at low tide, when many of its boats can be seen marooned on the Wye's muddy banks.

Beyond the bridge, where the road bends round to the left, look out for a wide metalled path that continues straight on. This climbs steeply uphill to a road, which you cross to pick up the path again on the other side. This becomes Mopla Road, a narrow lane which soon bends round to the right. Just in front of the first house on the left, the Offa's Dykes path leaves the road to climb into parkland. This is your route back, but for now, continue along the road until you reach a road junction, where you go straight on. Shortly, you make a right turn into Elm Road, where you immediately look for the Gloucestershire Way footpath which leaves the road on the left just in front of a bungalow. Walk down this path, which squeezes between the back gardens, to follow the left hand side of a small field. Go straight on here, to find a gate and stile leading you into the next field.

Walk up to the top right hand corner of the next field where you turn left onto a country lane. Within a short distance, turn right into Penmoel Lane and, at the end of this, look out for some steps off to the right which climb up a wall. At the top of these steps turn left to follow a narrow path which zig-zags up above Rock Cottage to reach a road. Turn left here and after a short distance look out for a path which leaves the road on the right under an arch. This is Moyle Old School Lane which eventually leads to the former school and its watchful owl.

Walk past the school and find a path that continues almost straight on; ignoring a metalled track which drops to the right and

Wintour's Leap

an indistinct path which heads off to the left near a large rusty gate.

Views now open up on both sides of this path; on your right is the River Severn, while on your left the Wye lies hidden under the rim of Woodcroft Quarry.

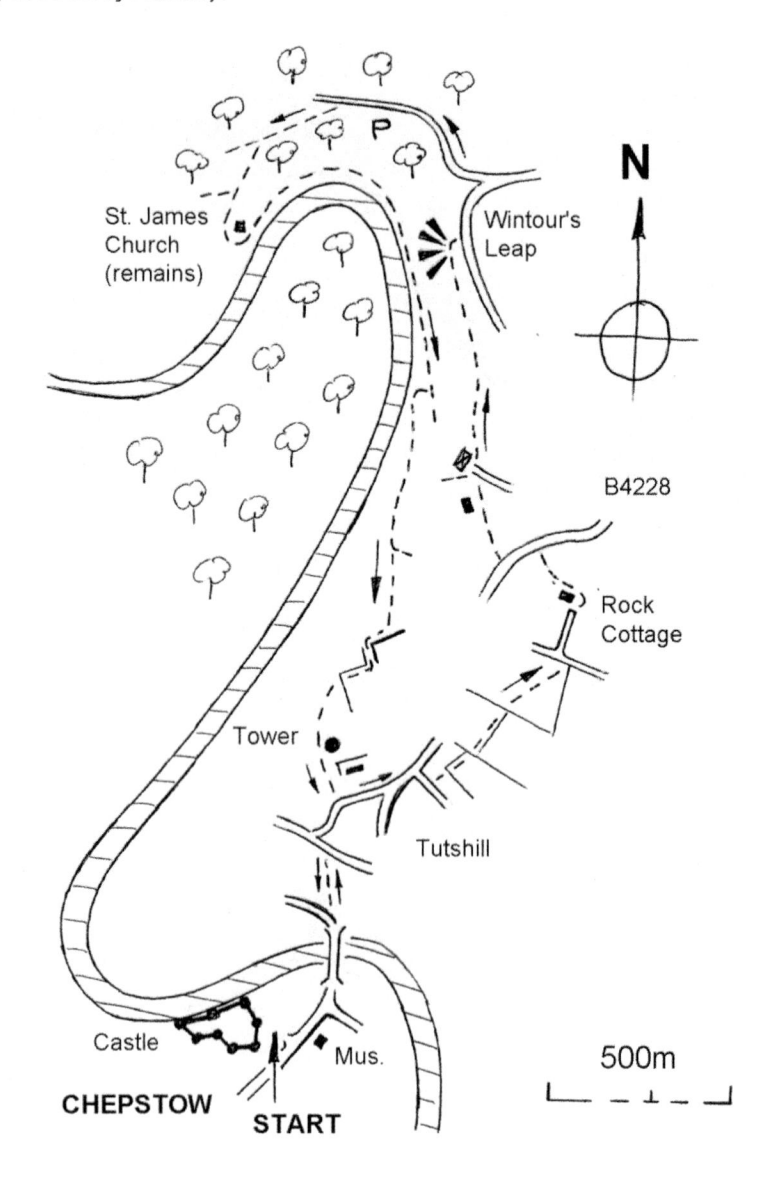

After passing through a kissing gate, the vegetation ominously begins to disappear on the left, and glimpses of the east bank of the Wye far below herald your imminent arrival at Wintours Leap. A couple of pieces of fencing protect you from the cliff edge to the left but, after these, a short path leads you to an unfenced viewpoint with a giddying drop of several hundred feet (for the faint hearted there is a safer viewpoint further ahead).

This is Wintours Leap; named after Colonel John Wintour, an unscrupulous industrialist and hardline royalist living in an area sympathetic to the Parliamentarian Cause. Legend has it that he was chased to this spot by Cromwell's troops during the civil war and, in a desperate bid to avoid capture, was supposed to have galloped over the cliff edge. The reality was somewhat different; Wintour managing to find his way down the cliff to board a royalist ship lying at anchor on the river below. He knew the area well but there appears to be no way down from here. Maybe he arrived with enough time to persuade a few locals to peer anxiously over the cliff while he hid nearby trying to calm his horse. Perhaps his pursuers simply lost the scent and invented the story to placate their angry superiors. I'll leave you to speculate!

Return to the path and follow it down to the road where you turn left. Almost immediately, a short path leads away from the road to a safer viewpoint. Continue along the road and as it begins a right turn, cross the road to take a path on the inside of the grass verge, which allows you to avoid on-coming traffic. At the end of the bend, cross the road again and turn left into Lancaut Lane.

Walk along the lane until, you reach a small car park near a Gloucestershire Wildlife Trust display board. About 250m beyond this turn left onto a path signposted 'Lancaut Church' and follow this path down through the woodland until a steeper path

Wintour's Leap

Wintour's Leap

appears on your left near an old limekiln.

Quarried limestone was burnt in the kiln to produce quicklime, to which water was added to make lime, a valuable product in agriculture and the construction industry.

Turn left here onto this path which drops steeply down to the river.

Soon the remains of St James's church come into view on the left and, beyond it, the limestone cliffs of the gorge rise dramatically above the trees.

Take a quick detour into the churchyard; here a display board tells the story of this 12th century church which occupies a delightful spot above a bend in the river. An unusually large number of medicinal herbs have been found in the church yard, including the non-native elecampane and green hellebore which supports a theory that the Lancaut peninsular was once home to a leper colony.

Leave the churchyard and walk down to the riverbank where you turn left under an ivy-clad ash tree.

The disturbed ground on the left was once Lancaut Quarry, where jetties were built to transport Stone down river. Quarrying became big business in this area with the opening of Bristol's Avonmouth Docks, which were built in 1877 to compete with facilities at Liverpool.

Follow the river as it reaches under the towering cliffs and battlements of Wintours Leap, where the path soon begins to climb away from the river into the trees. As the cliffs grow ever larger on the left, look out for a red arrow on a waymark post which directs you off the path and down to the river.

This path drops down through the trees and back up again to reach a boulder field. This obstruction resulted from a rock fall some years ago but fear not; just strike out across the boulders to where the path continues about 30 metres away on the other side. Yellow arrows may assist you in your quest.

Pat yourself on the back and continue along the path which climbs gradually up the side of the valley until it passes between a high wall and a wrought iron fence. Here the path begins to follow the wall round to the left, but your route is through a kissing gate on the outside of the bend, which allows you to go straight on across a meadow. Pass to the left of a solitary tree in the middle of the field before reaching a kissing gate on the far side. Turn right onto a driveway and follow the high wall on the left until, at its corner, you turn left near a doorway. Pass between two walls to reach a kissing gate where, ignoring a path that leads straight on, you turn sharp right to walk down the edge of a field bordered by pine trees and a stone wall. At the far end of this field, pass through another kissing gate and turn left, walking through a wooded glade to reach a ruined stone tower in the distance. As you walk across the grassy meadow, pass to the right of the old tower – once part of Chepstow's defensive perimeter – and begin a descent down to Mopla Road. Turn right here, and re-trace your steps back into the town centre, to reach the castle-side car park where you began the walk.

---------------------<{}>---------------------

My mum used to claim it was said
That brushing my teeth I did dread
Now my smile it is left
All alone and bereft
In a jar by the side of the bed

Walk 6: Piercefield

Soane's forgotten masterpiece

A walk packed with interest, which starts in the historic centre of Chepstow before reaching a ruined country estate. From there, the route passes through some delightful woodland along the top of the Wye gorge, to reach a memorable viewpoint. A long but gentle climb away from the town along paths which are good throughout.

Distance	3½ miles (5.5 km)
Route	Chepstow – Piercefield – Alcove Wood
Maps	OS Explorer Map OL14, and OS Landranger 162
Getting there	The walk starts from the Castle Dell Car Park in Chepstow
Start/Parking	The Castle Dell car park is next to the north east corner of Chepstow Castle. From outside the town, follow the signs to the town centre, and then to the castle itself
OS Grid Ref/Postcode	SO535942 / NP16 5GA

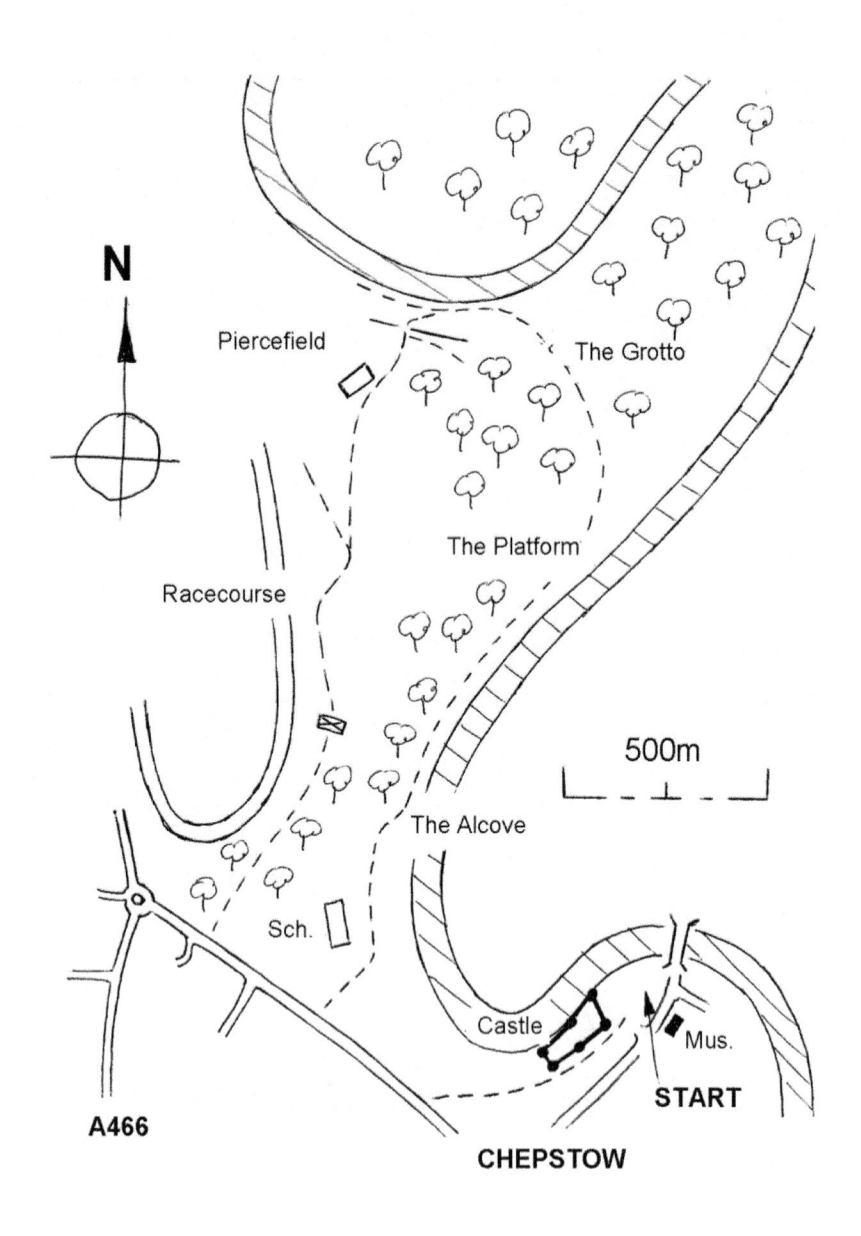

Piercefield

Piercefield

The walk
Head for the castle grounds, and look for a path which passes to the left of its tower and embankment.

The speed at which William the Conqueror committed himself to the construction of a castle here is a testament to its strategic importance. Construction began in 1067, and the castle defended the western border of his new kingdom from the troublesome welsh until the 15th century. A display board in the castle grounds gives more information on the history of Chepstow and its castle.

The path eventually climbs steeply away from the castle to reach a road beyond a wrought iron gateway. Turn right here, and follow the road up-hill for about 800m. Eventually, when you crest the top of the hill, look out for a drive on the right called 'The Cloisters'. Immediately beyond this, take a footpath which leaves the road to pass under a brick arch to reach some woodland. Follow the obvious route through the trees and shortly, when you reach a junction of paths, bear right onto a path which keeps to

Piercefield

the left of a stone wall. There are a number of small paths that wander off into the trees but they must all be ignored in favour of the wide and obvious path through the woodland. Eventually, as the railings of Chepstow Racecourse are glimpsed through the trees on the left, the path drops down to a five-bar gate.

Pass through this gate onto a gravelly track, which leaves the woodland behind to pass to the right of Chepstow Racecourse. Soon the track bears slightly right and in the distance can be seen the romantic ruin of Piercefield House. Further on, where the track bends to the left, a grassy path continues straight on, passing about 100m to the right of the house. This is your route, but pause here for a moment and look over your right shoulder for a dramatic view of the Severn Bridge, neatly framed between two oak trees.

Piercefield House, now an almost forgotten ruin, lies within the remains of Piercefield Park, once a 300 acre estate, which included the land now occupied by the race-course. The house dates back to Tudor times, and has passed through a number of hands including a sugar plantation owner and a self-made industrialist from the midlands; but the first of the two men to make an impact at Piercefield was Valentine Morris. He was the son of a Sugar plantation owner, and set about landscaping the grounds, creating features such as 'the grotto', 'the platform' and 'the alcove' so loved by the early Tourists (see walk 1). These were all sited high above the Wye valley, and enjoyed extensive views making Piercefield an unmissable attraction on the Wye Tour. He became governor of St Vincent but, after losing most of his money defending it against the French, he sold the house for £26,700 in 1784 to the other man to shape Piercefield – George Smith. The current appearance of the house is mostly the work of Sir John Soane who was commissioned by Smith to re-design the house. This resulted in a building similar to Shotesham in Norfolk, also Soanes work. It finally passed into the care of the Clay family who lived there until the death of Henry Clay in 1921, when it has since fallen into ruin.

Shortly after Clay's death, a consortium of ten worthy men from South Wales formed a company, which purchased the estate with the intention of building what is now Chepstow Racecourse. This opened in the summer of 1926, when over 20,000 race-goers turned up for the inaugural race meeting.

The racecourse was requisitioned early in the Second World War, and was used for the storage of Lancaster bombers prior to their entry into squadron service. The aircraft arrived by road on low loaders, and were assembled and parked under the trees. They were then flown across to Filton, near Bristol, using a grass runway constructed across the racecourse. This was an extremely hazardous exercise as the runway was too short but, with the aircraft stripped down to the bare essentials and only a pilot aboard, it was just possible with the undercarriage clipping the tree-tops behind you.

Immediately prior to D-Day, a US army battalion was stationed here under the command of Colonel Lucius Clay who, by a remarkable co- incidence, was descended from the last occupiers of the house. Part of their training included house-to-house fighting and Piercefield was utilised for this purpose using live ammunition, which did nothing to help the house's state of repair!

Turn off the track and take the path mentioned earlier, which passes close to the front of the house before passing through a copse, where it heads left to find a stile in a fence. Cross the stile and turn right, heading downhill for a short distance to meet the Wye Valley Walk. Turn right here, and follow this path along the top of the Wye gorge.

Piercefield

All three of Morris's landscape features have recently been restored and are found in this section of the walk. The first is 'the grotto', which soon appears on your right hand side.

Staying with the Wye Valley Walk you pass to the right of 'the platform', a dressed stone structure topped with iron railings, where a delightful view over the river must once have been enjoyed before trees obscured the view. After a while you reach 'the alcove', which affords a lofty view over the river and the nearby castle.

From here, walk uphill for a short distance, following the path as it turns left through a wall. Continue along this fenced pathway until you reach the car park of a Leisure Centre. Walk across this to reach the road where you turn left.

Retrace your steps back to the castle, being careful not to walk past the wrought iron gateway where you turn left into the castle grounds to reach your starting point in the car park.

The splendour of Piercefield was captured on canvas in 1840 by G Eyre Brooks. The painting hangs in Chepstow Museum, which is just across the road from the car park.

--------------------<{}>--------------------

My wife used to moan 'You have erred'
'in trying to have the last word'
If I really persist
With my will to resist
She will say 'I just never heard'

Walk 7: Doward

A walk back through time

A walk which starts in Symonds Yat West, and gradually goes back in time. Houses give way to ruins, well-tended gardens become lush, almost primeval forest, while further on the course of the virgin Wye is captured in limestone. Some careful navigation may be required in some places and the viewpoint is unfenced. One steady climb but paths are good throughout.

Distance	7.5 miles (12 km)
Route	Whitchurch – Symonds Yat – Biblins Bridge – Great Doward
Maps	OS Explorer Map OL14, and OS Landranger 162
Getting there	The walk starts at Symonds Yat West which lies just south of the A40 trunk road.
Start/Parking	Leave the A40 where signposted 'Whitchurch and Symonds Yat West' and head for the Old Court Hotel where roadside parking is available. Failing this, there is a 'pay-and-display' car park at Sterret's Caravan Park a few metres further on, just beyond the entrance to the Butterfly Zoo
OS Grid Ref/Postcode	SO554174 / HR9 6DA

The Walk

Walk into Sterret's Caravan Site, keeping to the left of it until you reach a two storey building. Pass to the right of this, and press on through the caravans for a short distance until you find the river bank. Turn right here, and follow the path along the river until you reach a gate on the far side of a gravelled area. Pass through the gate and continue alongside the Wye, which lies hidden behind the shrubbery, until you reach the car park of the Old Ferrie Inn.

Walk over to the Inn and look for a flight of stone steps half way along the building. It's remarkable how many people miss these steps and find themselves propped against the bar of this historic pub! The Inn served an important crossing point where the tow path changed banks to reach the shorter route on the inside of a great loop in the river. Climb up to the top of the steps and turn left onto a narrow lane.

Follow this for about 800m, passing through some woodland and alongside an old lime kiln before reaching a number of quaint riverside cottages at Symonds Yat West. On the opposite bank lies the Saracen's Head, which is reached by a hand-drawn ferry, summoned on demand by a bell at the riverside. Shortly after this, the narrow lane climbs away from the river and soon makes a sharp right turn. Look out for a track on the left here, which passes to the right of a telegraph pole before heading off towards 'The Old Pump House', a pretty holiday let. Beyond this, the track heads into the woodland where you take a right fork, ignoring the path on the left which drops down to the New Weir rapids, named after the forge that once existed next to the river here.

The River was once a busy trade route between Monmouth and Chepstow, and output from the forge would have been one of many cargos shipped downriver on boats which jostled for

Walk in the Wye Valley and Forest of Dean

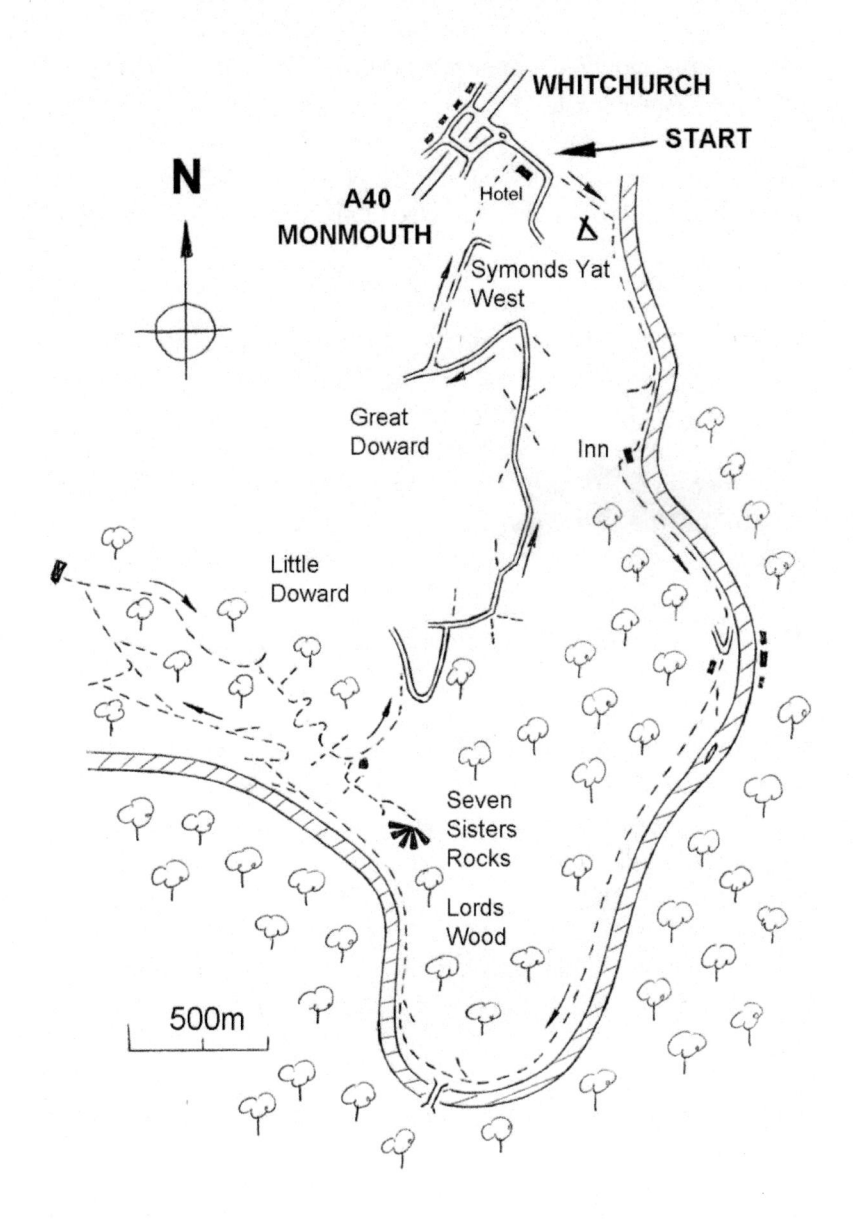

space on the crowded waterway with the early tourists doing the 'Wye Tour' (see walk 1).

Stay on the obvious path along the riverbank for 2 km to reach Biblins suspension bridge, passing along the way a number of caves, cliffs and old levels

Above the last cliffs before the bridge is the Dropping Wells Spring, which seeps down the face of the cliff. As the lime-rich water evaporates, it leaves a deposit of calcium carbonate over plant debris near the bottom, creating petrified leaves and twigs; a kind of 'instant fossil'. The bridge was built by the Forestry Commission in 1957 on the site of an aerial cable used to haul logs to the opposite bank for transport along a railway, which closed in 1964

Walk past the bridge and through the riverside meadow of the Biblins Campsite.

The campsite can be busy in the summer months acting as a home to a number of organised youth camps. Look down the valley here to see the Seven Sister Rocks, which stand high above the river. Later in the walk, you will be visiting the best of these for a bird's eye view of the gorge.

As the track bends right to reach a toilet block, continue straight ahead to reach the far corner of the meadow next to the river bank.

Follow the riverside path through the gloomy woodland which, in summer, has an almost primeval feel, thanks to the hart's tongue fern, which has colonised the woodland floor. The noise of the campsite disappears almost unnaturally quickly, to be replaced by an eerie silence broken only by your footfalls and the river lapping against the bank a metre away.

Stay with the riverbank for a while and, after passing a number of cliffs created by the river as it cut its gorge, you eventually arrive at a wrought iron gate standing between two stone columns. Walk to the left of this before arriving at a second iron gate a few metres further on. Follow the path beyond this using a wooden gate, ignoring a path which drops down to the river bank. Your path now climbs gradually away from the river for about 200metres to reach a logging track. Turn right here, and follow this track which climbs more steeply uphill until, where it makes a hair-pin left turn, a substantial old lime kiln can be seen on the right.

Following the restoration of the kiln in 2009, the method of operation can now be seen. Locally quarried limestone was carried to the top of the kiln, using the loading ramp on the left, to be roasted over the furnaces at the bottom to produce quicklime. This, combined with water, would produce slaked lime, which could be used as a soil improver or as a key ingredient in the production of cement.

Return to the path and continue uphill, wandering under the beech trees for about 600m after which a fence joins you on the left. Ignore a right fork which soon climbs away to the right and press on until you reach a junction with another track near a way-mark post marked with a red chevron. Turn right here, and climb up a steeply rising track which soon bends sharply left. A few metres further on, a grassy track drops down to join you from over your right shoulder. Ignore this, and continue on for a few more metres until, as the path levels out, you reach a junction of tracks. Turn sharp right, and follow this track which meanders underneath a limestone cliff shaded by mature beech trees, some of which have taken root in the limestone shelves by the path.

Eventually, a fence joins the path on the right, and you pass through a narrow canyon. As you emerge from this, cross a stile on the right (this was reported as missing recently but may have been re-instated), and walk down to a wall which is negotiated using a flight of steps. Continue beyond this and, ignoring a path which soon drops down from the left, follow the winding path downhill through the woodland. Eventually some open pasture is glimpsed through the trees on the left and, just as the path begins to climb again, it is crossed by another which reaches towards the edge of the pasture. Go straight ahead here and follow the path that now climbs up through the trees.

Shortly you reach a junction of paths near a way-mark post. Just ahead of you is King Arthur's Cave, partially hidden by a rise in the ground. The route continues to the left of the cave, but this post marks the point where you turn right, to make a short detour to the Seven Sisters Rock viewpoint.

Picnic on Seven Sisters' Rock!

The path to the viewpoint descends gently through the woodland before curving round to the left, where it is crossed by another. Go straight on here until, after about 300 metres, you reach a fork next to a way-mark post. Ignore the right fork which drops away into the woodland, in favour of a rocky path which climbs up to the left over a limestone outcrop. Follow this for about 100m until, after passing two way-mark posts, your reach a third, where a short path off to the right leads to the Seven Sisters Rocks. Yellow arrows on the trees confirm your route.

Judging by the number of feathers hereabouts, this airy viewpoint must be a popular lunchtime spot for kestrel, buzzard and peregrines. With a wisp of smoke from a camp fire, the secluded nature of the Biblins Campsite becomes all apparent, seemingly lost in a landscape of trees with only the Wye for company. Retrace your steps back to the cave, and follow a path that climbs gently uphill to the left of it.

King Arthur's cave dates back to the Ice Age, and a great variety of Palaeolithic hand tools and bones of long extinct animals (sabre toothed tiger, hyena, mammoth, lemming, etc) have been found here. Many of these finds are on display in Monmouth museum.

As you walk to the left of the cave, the path climbs past further hollows and arches, some of which clearly show signs of having been sculpted by water. This has in the past been attributed to the youthful Wye which was then just beginning to cut its gorge. More recent thought suggests that, as the ice sheet receded, a stream flowed down the pasture to the left, impacting against these cliffs and undercutting them.

The path eventually rises up to a road where you turn right. Follow this down to a hair-pin left bend, where it passes the entrance to the Doward Park Campsite. The road now climbs uphill, until it makes a junction with Leaping Stocks Road. Follow the narrow road round to the right, and stay on it for the next 1200m, as a number of green lanes join from both left and right, the first of these being May Bush Lane. After the last of these, Wye View Lane, the road begins to descend.

Doward

Eventually it makes a sharp left turn and further on, a telephone box and post box is seen on the right hand side of the road. Continue on for another 150metres and make a sharp right tun into Sawpitts Lane. Follow this road downhill as it passes a number of cottage driveways until it makes a sharp right turn onto Ashes Lane, where a view opens up over Symonds Yat West. Look to the left here for a kissing gate next to a driveway. Walk through this into a field and turn right, following the right hand boundary of the field down past some farm buildings, to reach the road and the start of the walk.

--------------------<{}>--------------------

When your memory's gone – every day is a new adventure.

Walk 8: Symonds Yat
One of England's finest views

The route takes you down a quiet wooded valley to follow the shaded riverside course of an old railway, before climbing steeply up to one of the Wye's many viewpoints. From here the route takes you through some delightful woodland where fallow deer may be seen. One steep climb, but paths are good throughout. Symonds Yat can be unbearably busy in summer so be sure to avoid peak times.

Distance	5½ miles (9 km)
Route	Bracelands – Biblins Bridge – Symonds Yat – Mailscot Lodge
Maps	OS Explorer Map OL14, and OS Landranger 162
Getting there	The walk starts at Bracelands Campsite which is 2 miles south of Symonds Yat
Start/Parking	From the A4136 at Five Acres, head north on the B4432 (signposted Symonds Yat). After about a mile, go straight over the crossroads onto Bracelands Drive. Follow this for about a mile until it finishes at the entrance to Bracelands Campsite. Park on the side of the road.
OS Grid Ref/Postcode	SO560131 / GL16 7NP

The walk

To the right, where the road finishes, is the entrance to Bracelands campsite but straight on a track can be seen beyond a forestry barrier.

Take this route and follow the track round for about 150m, until a short path off to the right allows access into the campsite beyond a gate. Opposite, a path drops away steeply into the trees. Turn left onto this, and walk downhill through the trees to reach a forestry track. Turn right here, and walk down a valley shaded by towering ash trees until, after about 1500m, you reach the river. Ignore the forestry track off to the right and continue on a few metres to find a riverside path on the right which passes between two boulders.

If time allows though, turn left and walk the short distance to Biblins Bridge, built by the Forestry Commission in 1957. The river bank on the other side of the suspension bridge is a lovely spot for a picnic.

Retrace your route back to the finger-post and, after passing between the two boulders, walk along the well-engineered path which is shaded by a wonderful variety of deciduous trees.

This path was the track-bed of the Ross to Monmouth Railway line which closed in 1965. Had it been able to survive for a few more years it would surely have been a candidate for preservation with a route that would put many of today's 'scenic' lines to shame.

Only recently have trees been allowed to grow at the waters' edge. The wye was once a busy trade route and the banks were originally cleared to allow men called bow hauliers to pull flat bottomed boats along the river. They were attached to the boats by a rope which they wore on a type of harness. Horses replaced men in the 19th century when the tow path was constructed. When steam trains arrived the risk of fire made it even more important to keep the vegetation clear.

Walk in the Wye Valley and Forest of Dean

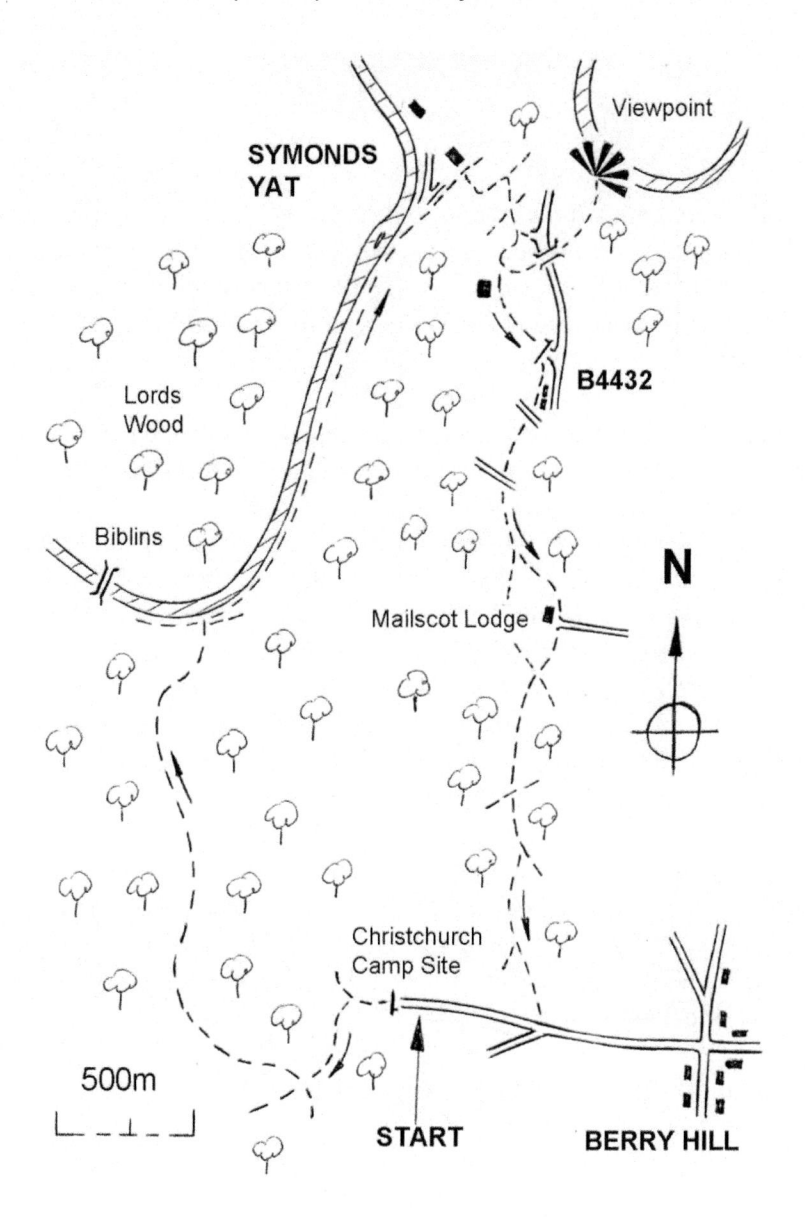

SYMONDS YAT

Viewpoint

Lords Wood

Biblins

B4432

Mailscot Lodge

N

Christchurch Camp Site

500m

START

BERRY HILL

Stay with the obvious path near the river and ignore any path that climbs away from it.

The old line is now perched on a ledge a few metres away from the Wye and, above the birdsong, the sound of rushing water heralds the approach of the New Weir rapids. On the opposite bank stood the New Weir iron works and, after its closure in 1798, the resulting slag was thrown into the river to create the island in the middle.

Continue past the rapids until, beyond a forestry barrier, you arrive at a car park, once the site of Symonds Yat Railway Station.

Pause at the far end of the car park where some platform edging stones can be seen beneath your feet. To the left, a narrow road leaves the car park and heads towards the Saracens Head and its rope-hauled ferry. Ahead of you is a hotel driveway, formerly the track-bed of the old railway line, which further on plunged into a tunnel. Hard to believe now but five trains a day passed through here. In the 1930's a camping coach (a specially converted old coach) was installed here for weekly hire.

Your route is a narrow path immediately to the right of the hotel driveway, sign-posted 'Yat Rock', which climbs up between a fence and a wall. Walk up this steep path from where, in winter, the tunnel portal can still be seen in the undergrowth between the path and hotel.

Eventually, a path appears on the right which climbs steeply up some steps. Turn onto this and begin a short but relentless climb up to Yat Rock. After a while, another junction of paths appear opposite a pair of gates. Turn sharp right here, and walk up a few steps to follow the path up through the beech trees. Go straight across a forestry track, which falls away to the right, and continue on up. After climbing up some stone steps, ignore a short path leading to the road in favour of a right turn up more steps, which take you to a grassy clearing near a log cabin. Look for a path off to the left which takes you over the road to the viewpoint.

Yat Rock, a limestone outcrop over 150m high, is one of the most celebrated views in England. The view extends in almost every direction above the river, which reaches under the towering cliffs of Coldwell Rocks before making a long horseshoe bend around the Huntsman peninsula. Yat Rock was once an Iron Age promontory fort, and there are remains of large banks and ditches around the log cabin. These are being cleared so that visitors can see them more easily. This was a popular stopping place for the 'Wye Tour' in the late 18th and early 19th centuries (see walk 1). The 'tourists' would disembark from their boat on the river below and make the steep climb up to this viewpoint. They would then walk down the path you just climbed up to rejoin their boat which, having travelled the four miles round the peninsula, was back within half a mile of where they had disembarked.

Peregrines have nested on the Coldwell Rocks for many years until the population was decimated by the effects of pesticides and robbery from the nests. Since 1982, the RSBP and the Forestry Commission, with the help of volunteers, have re-introduced the birds under a protection scheme, and powerful telescopes are available during the breeding season (April to August) for visitors to look directly into the nests.

Retrace your steps to the log cabin and, after walking past this, head left to pass through a small car park to reach a forestry barrier. Walk beyond the barrier to the main road. As you approach this, take a path on the right which runs parallel with the road for a while before passing behind a couple of cottages.

Symonds Yat

View from Symonds Yat Rock

Soon a narrow metalled road is crossed, and further on the path crosses a second road guarded by forestry barriers. Eventually the path forks under an old oak tree where you head left, ignoring the more obvious path which descends gently to the right. The path soon begins to climb towards Mailscot Lodge where, ignoring the driveway to the left, you walk past its front gate and slightly right, onto a path which drops gently through the trees.

This is a wonderful part of the walk along a path which passes under the overhanging boughs of up to 20 different tree species. Herds of deer are often heard before they are seen here, your sudden arrival sparking the gentle drumming of hooves as they make their escape into the trees.

On the next section, keep straight on along the obvious path in front of you. Further on you cross a track which heads towards a cottage beyond a forestry barrier. Still further another track crosses your path to dip under a power line. A couple more minor paths tempt you off to the left until you eventually reach a fork under a beech tree where you bear right. Later, after ignoring a path which drops to the right, you climb up past an adventure centre to reach Bracelands Drive which lies just beyond a forestry barrier. Turn right here and walk back to the start.

--------------------<{}>--------------------
Your lack of planning becomes my rush job.

Walk 9: Coppet Hill

A medieval 'weapon of mass destruction'

Coppet Hill is almost cast adrift in an enormous loop in the River Wye and this walk takes in the fine views that can be enjoyed from its summit ridge. The walk returns along the bank of the Wye after visiting what must surely be the most tranquil spot in its entire length. There are a couple of steep hills but paths are good throughout.

Distance	6½ miles (10.5 km)
Route	Goodrich – Coppet Hill – Welsh Bicknor
Maps	OS Explorer Map OL14, and OS Landranger 162
Getting there	The walk starts from Goodrich which is 4 miles south west of Ross on Wye
Start/Parking	Park in the village near the school, in a lay-by used by parents doing the 'school run'. Provided you don't use it early morning or late afternoon on schooldays, parking here will be quite straightforward. Failing this, there are a number of other places nearby where a car can be left
OS Grid Ref/Postcode	SO575193 / HR9 6HY

The Walk

Leaving the school, walk up to the road junction where you take a right turn onto a lane that climbs away from the village in a south easterly direction signposted Courtfield and Welsh Bicknor. Ahead of you at this junction is the lane leading to Goodrich Castle, a fine example of a marcher castle guarding the border between Wales and England

Walk up the hill, passing over what the locals call the 'Dry Arch' – presumably because it spans a road and there is no water beneath it.

The road was constructed as a toll road in 1828 to give local coal and iron ore a more direct route to South Wales, thus avoiding a longer and more expensive journey through Ross.

Continue up the hill to reach a fork in the road where, on your left, the elegant arches of Kerne Bridge can be seen, one of loveliest on the Wye.

It was built at the same time as the road, and a toll was collected here until the 1950s when the gate and toll keepers cottage were removed. The bridge replaced an earlier ferry sited near the castle, and it was while using this in 1387 that King Henry IV heard of the birth of his son, the future victor of Agincourt. The King was so overjoyed he gave the startled ferryman the revenue of the ferry in perpetuity.

To the left of the bridge lies a development of holiday apartments which were adapted from farm buildings in the early 1980s. These were built on the site of the former Flanesford Priory, which housed an Order of Augustinian Monks until the Dissolution of the Monasteries act in 1537. The refectory in the long barn and the fish pond are all that remain of the Priory, which was founded in 1346.

Returning to the road junction, take a path that leaves the top side of a green triangular road island and climb steeply up the hillside. After rising up through the trees, the path clings to the side of the steeply sloping ridge and to your right, all gathered around the church as if to keep warm, lies the village of Goodrich.

During the Civil War the vicar was The Reverend Thomas Swift, an ardent Royalist, and grandfather of Jonathan Swift, author of Gulliver's Travels.

Near the top of the climb you emerge onto Coppet Hill, which has been coppiced since the Iron Age to provide charcoal for iron smelting. Limestone was quarried for many years to aid the smelting process and to improve the soil. For centuries the land belonged to Goodrich Manor, but since 1920 has been owned by a charitable trust of which many of the residents, especially of the older properties, are trustees.

Its status as a nature reserve recognises the diversity of flora and fauna which exist here, which include species of national importance. On the ground the alkaline soils support a range of orchids including the common spotted, white helliborine, greater butterfly, and early purple, while a more widespread plant is the meadow saffron with its light purple flowers. These unusual plants produce flowers without leaves in the autumn, giving them the name 'Naked Ladies'; the leaves and seed-pod appearing in the spring. Frequently seen in the skies over the hill are kestrel, goshawk, sparrow hawk, and hobby. In the woods there is a nest box scheme which attracts blue tits, coal tits and great tits. There are also long-tailed tits, nuthatches, tree creepers and the greater spotted and green woodpeckers. The common has a relatively high population of adders, so be wary of straying from the path.

Walk in the Wye Valley and Forest of Dean

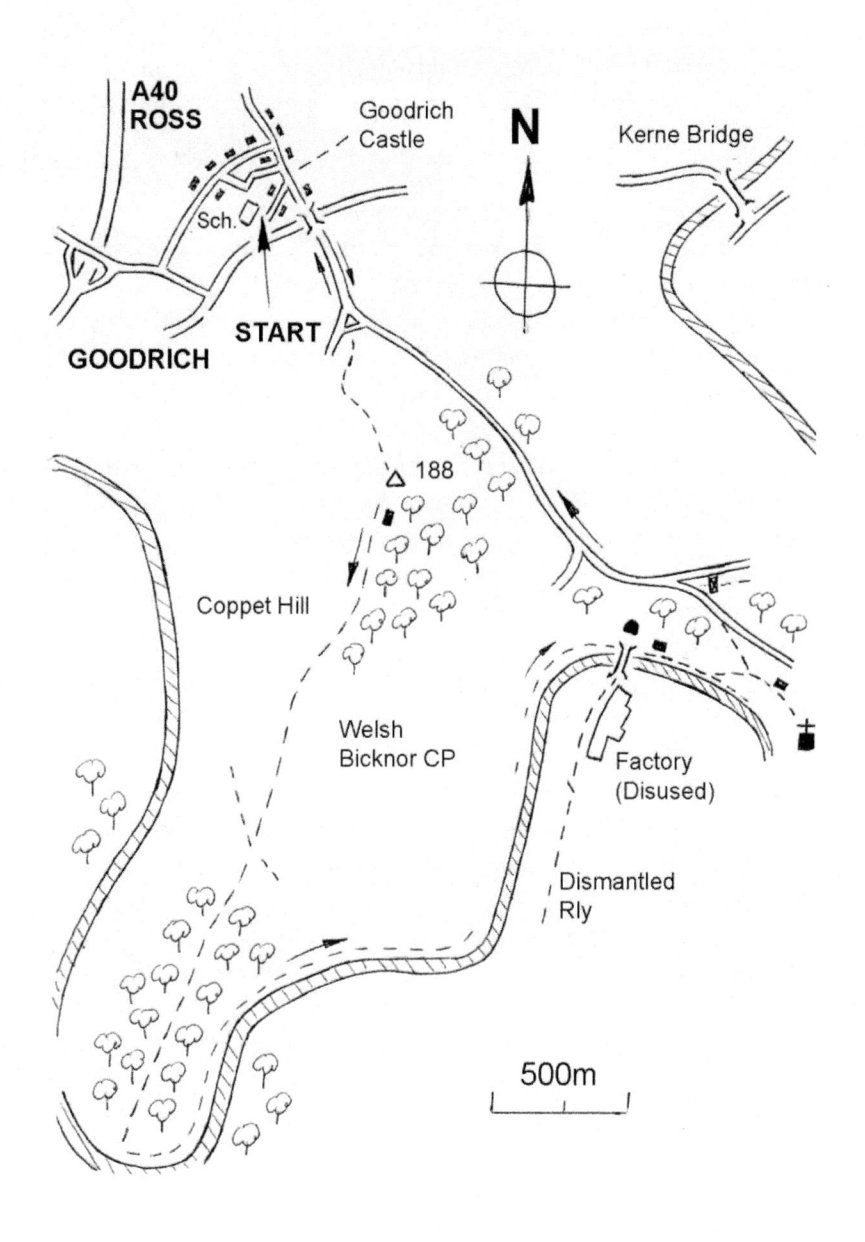

Coppet Hill

If you're feeling a bit weary after the climb, then maybe the surveyor did as well, because unusually the trig point is just below the summit, which is further up to the right near a ruin known locally as 'the folly'.

This is most likely to have been the residence of a warriner, charged with the task of managing the rabbits, which were probably introduced to the hill by the Normans.
Pause for a moment and look back the way you came. Just beyond the village, standing malevolently on its' high rocky bluff, stands Goodrich Castle.

Dating back to the 11th century, the Castle commanded an ancient crossing point of the Wye, known as Walesford (now Walford), which separated England from Wales. It remained impregnable for over 500 years before being the subject of a desperate siege in the civil war by Parliamentary forces under the command of Colonel Birch. Despite a long campaign of attrition, he was unable to breach the walls of the fortress; so Parliament asked Birch to commission a new type of giant mortar which was cast locally. With a barrel diameter of 400mm, 'Roaring Meg' was the largest mortar firing the biggest cannon balls in the world. Birch returned to Goodrich with his 'wonder weapon' and was so excited that he insisted on firing the opening shots himself! The 100kg shells soon penetrated the castle walls and the Royalists were forced to surrender. The mortar stood for many years in the city of Hereford, but is now on display in the castle, which is well worth a visit.

There is a sad footnote to this final act. During the siege Alice Birch, Colonel Birch's niece, infiltrated the castle defences to join her lover, royalist Charles Clifford. When it was apparent that the castle would fall they fled on Clifford's horse, breaking through the parliamentary lines during a storm, only to drown while crossing the swollen Wye. It is said that on stormy nights their cries can still be heard over the rushing river.

Return to the walk and climb up to the edge of the woodland before passing to the right of the ruined cottage. Keep the woodland on your left and follow the clear path along the ridge. Just inside the woodland is an old boundary wall which keeps you company all the way down to the river.

To your right, the mirror-smooth Wye passes under the slender steel frame of Huntsham Bridge; its lazy bend leads your eye towards the village of Symonds Yat, which nestles at the entrance to the Wye gorge. Above you, the mewing 'kiew' call of a soaring buzzard may alert you to its presence, while on the breeze the familiar coconut scent of the gorse completes the sensory experience.

Eventually your route burrows downhill through an overgrown hazel coppice where, if you are quiet, you may literally bump into an unsuspecting fallow deer. The wall has now become a tumble of moss- covered boulders lying, in late spring, amongst a carpet of bluebells.

Eventually you emerge from the shadows onto a broad swathe of grassy riverbank in front of the towers and battlements of Coldwell Rocks, famous as the nesting site of a number of peregrine falcons.

High up to your right can be seen the bustling tourist magnet of Symonds Yat Rock, where the RSPB operate a falcon observation post during the nesting season. Down here you will linger, almost certainly alone, to enjoy the timeless charm of this idyllic spot, naively imagining that you had just discovered it all for yourself.

Turn left and, with the river on your right, drag yourself away to follow the riverbank until the woodland rushes down again to meet you near a gate. Go through the gate and walk along a broad track which shortly passes to the right of a memorial.

This memorial was erected in memory of John Whitehead Warre, a 15 year old boy who drowned at this spot in 1804 while accompanying his parents on the 'Wye Tour' (see walk 1). He unwisely went for a swim too soon after the substantial lunch provided by the boat operator, got cramp and drowned.

At the end of this woodland section the river passes through some pasture land, and your route takes you along the river bank through five fields before the trees close in again.

This section of the Wye is a popular route for canoeists on their way to the rapids just below Symonds Yat. Just after you enter the woodland, the path is the subject of a diversion by the county council but you are soon back enjoying the view from the river bank. The rather incongruous 30 acre industrial complex on the other side is a now disused factory, which was originally built in 1912 to produce cable and wire. The site expanded rapidly and over 1,200 people were employed at its peak but, after the Second World War, the isolated nature of the site became a factor and the works closed in 1965 leaving 840 people unemployed. The closing of the railway line in the same year meant that this loss was keenly felt. A reprieve arrived the following year when the site was open again making packaging for products as diverse as chocolate and televisions, but after production moved to Newport in 2002 the factory finally closed, seemingly for good.

Soon you pass underneath an old railway bridge which carried the Ross to Monmouth line over the river. This is now a footbridge from which can be seen the southern portal of the tunnel taking the line under Coppet Hill.

Kerne Bridge

Just after passing to the right of a cottage you reach a clear fork in the path. Bear left here, climbing away from the river, before taking a steep left turn up a flight of steps just before Welsh Bicknor Youth Hostel. This is your route but, if time allows, walk a few metres further on past the hostel, originally a Victorian rectory, to reach the pretty church of St Margaret's.

St Margaret's was built in 1858 on the site of a medieval church but is no longer in use.

Retrace your steps back past the hostel and climb up the steps of the path which rises steeply through the trees to reach a narrow lane. Turn left here and follow the lane until it emerges on open pasture near the top of the hill. Follow the lane as it bends gradually right, ignoring another lane which joins from the left. As you re-enter the woodland on the north side of the hill, look out for the views which open out again to Kerne Bridge and the Wye valley. Follow the road back down into the village.

Walk 10: Lydbrook
A star of the West End

The walk takes you high up the east side of the Lyd valley along old railway lines, before making a lonely sojourn through some of the quietest woodland in the forest. The return high up the west side of the valley offers rewarding views and glimpses of some of Lydbrook's listed buildings.

Distance	7 miles (11 km)
Route	Lydbrook – Sallowvalets – Hangerberry Hill
Maps	OS Explorer Map OL14, and OS Landranger 162
Getting there	The walk starts at Lower Lydbrook on the B4234
Start/Parking	Park at a small car park next to the River Wye near the junction of the B4228 and B4234
OS Grid Ref/Postcode	SO596169 / GL17 9NW

Lydbrook

For most of its history Lydbrook has been a hive of industrial activity thanks to its close proximity to timber, stone, coal and iron ore. The fast flowing Lyd Brook was harnessed to power its mills, and it enjoyed good communications and transport links via the Wye. It became the principle coal port on the river from which Forest coal was shipped to Ross and Hereford.

A mill existed at Lydbrook as early as 1282 and, by the late 15th century, there were a number of furnaces, forges and lime kilns. These early industries were, in turn, replaced in the 19th century by a wireworks, a tinplate works and associated rolling mills. At the time the coal industry was growing fast and Lydbrook had a number of collieries, the largest of which occupied a site high up the valley. Much of the output was carried away on a tramway and a later railway which leapt across the valley on a slender viaduct. These indigenous industries declined as the 20th century wore on, to be replaced by newer industries which were more volatile, simply tapping in to the ready supply of labour. The sprawling industrial site half a mile west of the car park was originally a cable works which, until 2002, had been adapted to produce packaging for products as diverse as televisions and chocolate; but even this has now fallen silent, seemingly for good.

The village is now a tranquil backwater, and surprisingly little of its industrial history remains to be seen. The area of the village nearest the Wye is a conservation area and contains a number of listed buildings.

The walk
Turn left out of the car park and cross the road, looking for a long flight of steps immediately to the right of a cream coloured cottage. These take you up past the abutments of the old viaduct which carried the railway 30 metres above the road below.

It was built by the Severn and Wye Railway in 1872 and was a major feat of Victorian engineering, but was sadly dismantled in 1965 for safety reasons following the closure of the railway in the 1950s.

At the top of the steps you reach a broad track which was the terminus of the earlier tramway built in 1812.

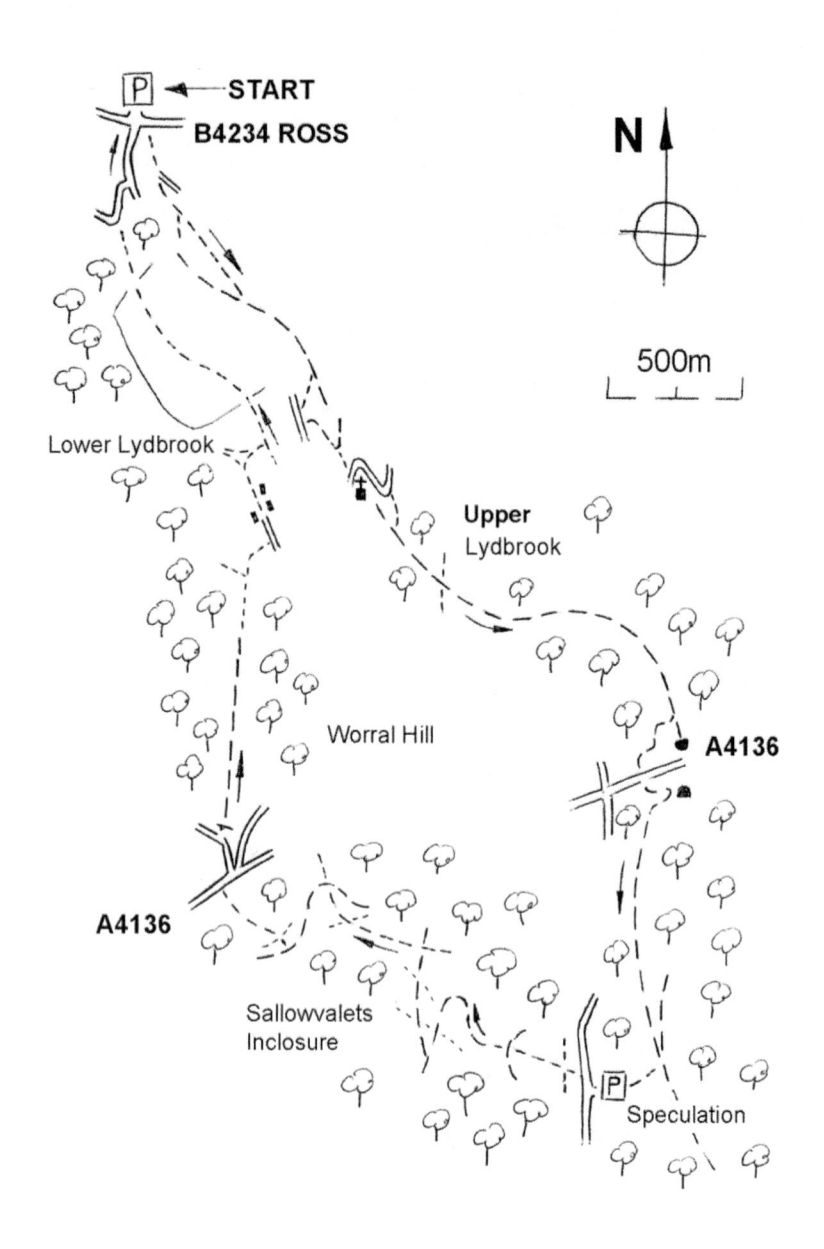

Lydbrook

From here, goods were lowered down a rope worked incline to reach a small dock at the side of the river.

Ignore the road and fork right, following the route of the old tramway, which soon passes to the right of the aptly named Incline Cottage. Ignore a broad path which drops down to the right, and continue straight ahead past a lovingly restored old chapel

This was the last of seven church buildings built in Lydbrook, and was well attended before the congregation declined to a point where only occasional services were held. Eventually the building fell into disuse, finally closing in 1980.

Continue along the path, which now becomes a leafy bower carpeted in spring by bluebells and wild garlic. Eventually the route of the old tramway becomes obstructed, but luckily some steps drop down to the right to reach the old railway. Walk down these steps and turn left. Continue along the track-bed until a retaining wall appears on the left opposite a path which drops down to the valley floor.

This path served the white house visible above the wall, and was obstructed, not once but twice when first the tramway and then, at a slightly lower elevation, the railway passed close by. On each occasion an archway and flight of steps were built into the retaining walls to allow the occupants to reach the house. The second arch and steps are a few metres above you, out of sight next to the route of the tramway. Small wonder that when the railway closed, the occupier applied for permission to use the track bed ahead (complete with tunnel!) as a private drive.

Take the path that drops to the right here, and follow it down to reach a car park by the main road through the village. Turn left onto the road, and after passing the Prince of Wales, one of Lydbrook's many former inns, look out for a telegraph pole near a steel railing. Immediately after this, turn left onto a rough

Lydbrook

track and follow it away from the road for a few metres before turning right, staying with the track as it climbs gently uphill. Further up, where it doubles back on itself, take a footpath straight on that leads towards the church.

This is the Church of Holy Jesus, and although it opened as long ago as 1851, it had to wait 140 years for a proper water supply – this no doubt made christening ceremonies easier! Nothing is wasted here, stone from the dismantled viaduct finding its way into the graveyard walls.

Turn left onto the road in front of the church, and follow it as it immediately turns right to climb up towards a sharp left hand bend. At the apex of the bend, turn right onto a path that zig-zags down through pine trees to reach the track bed of the old railway.

This part of the route is shared with cyclists, the track being part of a network of cycle trails which follow the area's many disused railway lines.

Turn left onto this and follow this track which affords ample views into the valley on the right.

Eventually, across a paddock on the left, the original vicarage can be seen. This was cut off from the church by the arrival of the railway and the vicar was given permission, on Sundays only, to walk along the line to reach his flock.

After passing over a trestle bridge, the path leaps across the Greathough brook on an embankment before crossing two further trestle bridges.

After the third trestle bridge, take a path which forks right, leaving the old railway line to zig-zag up through the conifers to reach the busy A4136. After carefully crossing the road, take the path opposite, and follow it as it turns left then right through a plantation of conifers. The path then broadens out and continues past a substantial old bridge on the left, before rejoining the track bed of the old railway. After passing through a substantial cutting shaded by beech and oak, the path reaches a junction of paths overseen by a cycleway finger post. Leave the track here and turn right, walking down through the trees into the Speculation Picnic Area.

The picnic area lies on the site of the similarly named colliery which was an early effort to reach the deeper reserves of coal in the Forest. Almost nothing remains now except for a partly filled in shaft, which is visible in the corner of the meadow surrounded by wire fencing.

Walk through the picnic area and down to the road where you turn right, looking for a footpath which leaves the road on the left after about 50 metres.

Follow this path through the woodland, going straight ahead at a crossroads of paths and again further on, where a broad forestry track makes a sweeping curve in front of you. The path now climbs up through the trees accompanied on the left by a brook carried in a man-made water channel or 'leat'.

Mining activities in the Forest have always been hampered by the excessive amounts of water found underground which required a substantial investment in pumping machinery to remove. The underlying strata here is pervious limestone, and the trough was almost certainly constructed to minimise the seepage of water into the mine workings below.

After a while an inviting stone bridge tempts you down to the left, but stay with the broad path as it climbs up through the trees. The track finally swings left to pass over the leat before levelling out in a wonderfully quiet area of woodland. There are a number of

Lydbrook

biking trails ahead which must be ignored in favour of the broad track you are on. This soon meets another broad track where you turn right -almost doubling back on yourself. Follow this until you meet a junction of paths just beyond a stream. Turn left here to follow the stream up through the fir trees. Eventually you meet a broad forestry track where you turn left. This bends left and then right as it levels out near the top of the valley. As you round the second bend, look out for a path which leaves the inside of the bend on the right. Turn onto this path which soon bends slightly left to tunnel through a dense plantation of spruce. This is the Wysis Way with its orange waymark posts. As you approach the A4136 let the traffic noise guide you through a maze of bike trails before emerging onto the road.

New arrivals in Sallowvalets

At the road, take the first of the two lanes opposite you signposted Eastbach. After a short distance, turn right onto a forestry track and after rounding the barrier, follow the long straight track beyond it through the woodland. Eventually, after a clearing, the track narrows to a path which can be a little overgrown in summer. Soon another path drops down to join you from the left, but keep straight on and, after passing under a power line, you begin to descend through the pine trees. Follow the path steeply down to a lane where you turn left.

Directions have to be followed carefully now.
Stay with this lane for about 100m until, where the tarmac ends, you climb up a rough driveway.
After about 50m, look for a path which climbs up to the left in order to pass behind a cottage.
This path occupies a narrow ledge before beginning a steep drop through some beech trees and the walls of a number of long abandoned dwellings.
After levelling out a bit the path bends down to the right to reach an indistinct cross-roads. Turn left here, ignoring a path which continues on down into the valley.
After about 100m you leave the woodland behind and pass through a steel gate. Follow the path across an open meadow, aiming to the left of an oak tree in the middle distance.

Pause for a moment and look down at an old house on the nearside of the road. This magnificent 16th century house is reputed to have been the childhood home of the famous 18th century actress Sarah Siddons. The house contains many original features including the timber framing, a timber Tudor arch to the rear porch, a double boarded timber front door, some original 6 and 9 light mullion windows, a spiral oak staircase, and substantial areas of wattle and daub panelling in the roof and rear wall. The main downstairs room has an almost complete 17th century panelled interior with a plastered ceiling featuring fruit and foliage. Its interior retains many of the original oak doors and latches.

As a child, Sarah Siddons worked as an actress in her father's small troupe of travelling actors, her precocious talent eventually getting her an opportunity at the Drury Lane Theatre in London. Owing to inexperience and other circumstances her debut was not a success. Undeterred, she returned to tour the provinces where she earned a reputation as a queen of tragedy, eventually earning another chance at Drury Lane seven years later. This time she was a phenomenal success, and for the next 20 years was the undisputed diva of the West End even giving the royal children elocution lessons – not bad for a girl born a few miles away in Brecon!

The path keeps to the left of a power line for a distance until, as more woodland approaches, it reaches a gate where the line enters the woodland. After passing through this gate, follow the path down to a narrow lane. Turn right here and walk down the lane, which falls steeply towards its junction with the main road near a timbered house called 'The Priory'.

This is a haunted house with a secret room. It is the oldest of Lydbrooks' listed buildings dating back to the 14th century.

Turn left at the road and walk through the village towards the riverside car park at the start of the walk

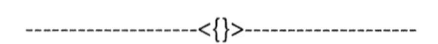

--------------------<{}>--------------------

Work for as long as you can – the mortality rate of those who retire is very high indeed.

Walk 11: Ruardean Hill

An anxious wait!

Highlights of this walk are some splendid woodland and an outstanding view from Ruardean Hill which overlooks the Wye valley and distant South Wales. The walk passes high above the village of Ruardean which is well worth a visit. One or two steep sections but paths are good throughout.

Distance	5 miles (8 km)
Route	Brierley – Horse Lea – Ruardean Hill – Ruardean Woodside
Maps	OS Explorer Map OL14, and OS Landranger 162
Getting there	The walk starts near Brierley on the A4136 road
Start/Parking	There are two minor roads that leave the north side of the A4136 at Brierley. Take the road signposted 'The Pludds' and follow it down through the trees for about a quarter mile until you reach a forestry track on your left. Park near the forestry gate
OS Grid Ref/Postcode	SO621154 / GL17 9DL

Ruardean

The walk

Walk around the forestry barrier and, ignoring the path that climbs away to your left, take the obvious track which is soon accompanied on the left by the Greathough Brook. After a long left-hand bend fork right onto a track which climbs steeply out of the valley.

Eventually, after the gradient has eased a little, you begin a sharp left-hand bend. Half way around this bend, look for a footpath off to the right, which climbs up through the trees. Walk up this path until you reach the edge of the woodland, beyond which can be seen some pasture land and the scattered settlement of The Pludds. Turn left here, and climb up through some magnificent mature oak trees, passing a path which joins from the left, to reach a forestry track where you turn left. Follow this broad track through the woodland in a south-westerly direction for about 300 metres until you reach a junction of tracks. Your route here is straight on but, for the moment, take a forestry track on the left which tunnels through a dense stand of conifers to reach a sunlit spot in the trees.

Pludds Colliery Memorial Stone

Make your way over to a memorial stone near the site of an old mine shaft, which was filled in to ground level in 2008 for safety reasons.
In 1949 this was the site of a dramatic escape from a colliery in nearby Lydbrook, which flooded suddenly one morning. Most of the 150 miners rushed towards the main shaft where they were struck by a wall of water which swept them off their feet. Clinging to pipes and cables, they struggled back towards the main shaft through waist deep swirling water, some reaching it with only their heads above the torrent. The pit ponies were drowned but last man up rescued the pit cat which had never seen daylight. A count on the surface revealed that five men were still missing. One of these, George Manwaring, was leaving the mine, but turned back when he discovered that an elderly colleague was in difficulties. He went back to find him knowing that he might never reach the surface again. He found his colleague and two others who were trying to get another elderly miner out. The three men slowly inched their way towards the main shaft, supporting and carrying their older colleagues. En route they found a working telephone, and called the surface with the news that they were still alive. They were told that the flood water was now 5 metres deep at the bottom of the main shaft and that they were completely cut off.

Their only chance of escape was to crawl through a long forgotten labyrinth of workings and galleries to the bottom of the shaft you see at your feet. The three men set off through the dark flooded galleries, taking with them their two older colleagues, one of whom was completely exhausted and had to be carried most of the way. Meanwhile, rescuers here set up a winch, and lowered a large bucket 130 metres down this old shaft and began a long and anxious wait. Morning turned into afternoon and evening beckoned when suddenly there was a tug on the rope. The men's journey had been hard, the route tortuous and the air rank and suffocating but they had succeeded in reaching the bottom of this shaft. The older men were hauled up to safety first, followed by the rest of the party, to be warmly greeted by their relieved families. In 1975 the three men were awarded the Edward Medal for their bravery in risking their lives to save others. Manwaring later made a journey to Buckingham Palace to have the George Cross conferred upon him by the Queen.

Retrace your steps back to the track and take the path mentioned earlier, now a left turn, ignoring a couple of paths opposite you which climb away through the woodland.

Continue along this undulating path which eventually passes under a power line until, immediately after passing under a second power line, you reach a junction of tracks in front of a mature oak. Go straight ahead here, passing to the right of the oak tree to reach a roadside cottage about 100m further on. Turn right on reaching the lane and begin a gentle up-hill climb.

The second house on the left was formerly the Mason Arms; its missing pub sign a poignant reminder of the many pubs that have closed in recent times.

Bear right at a fork in the road and follow the lane as it climbs more steeply up Ruardean Hill.

Breath-taking views open up to the left of the Wye valley and in particular the river, which plays hide and seek as it loops in and out of view nearly 300 metres below. Beyond, the vista stretches as far west as the Brecons in Wales, and as far north as Clee Hill in Shropshire.

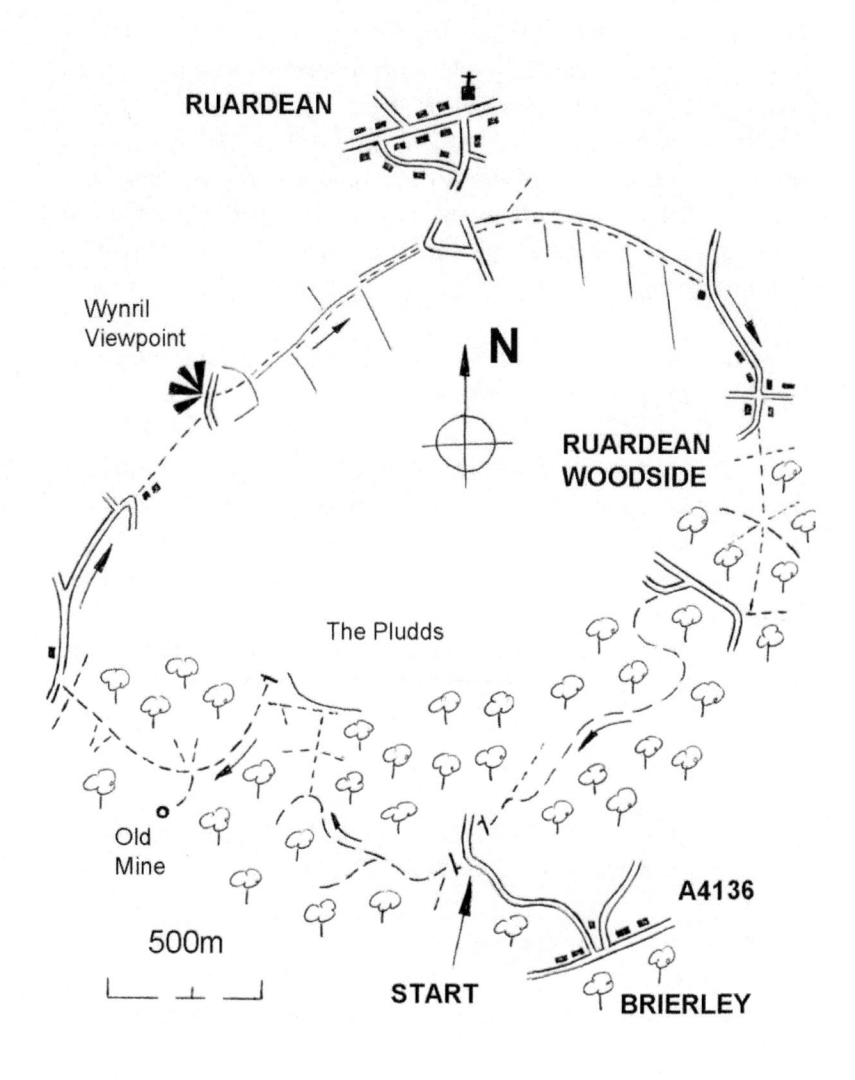

Walk in the Wye Valley and Forest of Dean

Continue your steep climb up the lane until, just beyond another left turn, the road bends sharply right, almost doubling back on itself near a row of cottages. Leave the road here and follow the bridleway to the left of the cottages; the last one having a delightful privy at the bottom of the garden. Follow the holly and willow shaded bridleway until it eventually reaches a road, where a left turn takes you immediately to the Wynril Viewpoint with its immense views.

Here an engraved plate atop a plinth names all the mountains visible on the horizon.

Cross the road and look for a footpath finger-post that directs you up over a stile and into a field. From here, take a left diagonal and look for another stile in the left-hand boundary of the field around 150 metres away. Cross the stile and continue to the corner of this field keeping the hedgerow on your right. Another stile in the corner takes you to the other side of the hedge which you now keep on your left until a further stile leads you onto a bridleway, once an old lane that gave access to the many mine workings hereabouts.

This area was once a rough wasteland disfigured by spoil tips and old mine workings which spread over the hillside.

Follow the bridleway until you reach a road. Bear slightly right here along Pettycroft, a line of cottages built in the late 1860s almost certainly to house mine workers from nearby pits.

If time allows, the village of Ruardean is well worth a visit, reached by turning left here onto Kingsway Lane which drops steeply down into the heart of the village.

Little now remains of the Ruardean's industrial history, but once it was a busy industrial centre with furnaces, forges and coal mines. The dining room of The Malt Shovel Inn is notable for having windows somehow acquired from No. 10 Downing Street, while close by an old granary was the site where an alternative brew was made to that on offer in the pub. Here James and William Horlick conducted experiments blending malt and dried milk, which later became the world famous drink that bears their name. The church of St John the Baptist dates back to the twelfth century; the larger nave, chancel, tower and spire being 14th century additions to the original Lady Chapel. Notable features of the church consist of a carving of the Virgin Mary over the south porch, and a tympanum representing St. George and the Dragon above the south door, dated to the 12th century and carved by the Hereford School of Sculpture. In the bell tower there is a painting of the tympanum, and inserted in the wall to the left of the front door is a small carving of fish also dating from the 12th century; this was truly lost and found, being rediscovered in a local cottage in 1985 after being missing for 800 years! On a spur north-west of the church are the remains of an old manor house and castle, now little more than a mound, which commanded the shortest route from Gloucester to the Welsh Marches and the Wye valley. Known locally as The Castle, it was reputedly destroyed during the Civil War.

Retrace your steps up the steep climb to 'Pettycroft' and, after pausing for breath, follow the road which eventually arrives at a T-junction. Turn left here onto Turners Tump, and walk down this lane for a few metres until a driveway leaves the road on the right. Just before this, turn right onto a slightly overgrown path that climbs steeply away from the road. Cross the stile at the top and keep to the right of the hedge for the next five fields, ignoring a kissing gate in the first field that leads down to the left.

To your right the former colliery village of Ruardean Woodside spreads itself across the hillside as if trying to rise above the forest, which extends from the horizon to the village like an incoming tide.

Avoid the temptation to stray downhill and, after hugging the hedge on your left, you finally arrive at the corner of the fifth field where, next to a whitewashed house, a stile takes you onto a lane. Turn right here and follow the lane into Ruardean Woodside where, after going straight over a crossroads, the approaching trees signal an end to dramatic views and an imminent plunge into the darkness of the forest.

As the road as it turns sharply right, take a path on the left which continues straight on into the trees.

Follow the path which descends through mixed woodland eventually reaching a junction of six paths; the widest of which sweeps across in front of you. Maintain your bearing and cross this wide path, ignoring two routes on the left and two on the right, before continuing downhill through the trees. The path eventually makes a T-junction where you turn right. Follow this path for a short distance down to a road where you turn right to walk towards Ruardean Woodside, passing on your left an old spoil tip now clothed in conifers. Just before the village, take a left turn signposted Newham Bottom. After about 200m, leave the road as it bends to the right, and follow a track which goes straight on into the trees. Walk down through the conifers on a broad path that eventually becomes a well-made forest track. This meanders downhill for some way until crossing the Greathough Brook where another track joins from the right. Continue downhill with the brook now on your left until you reach a forestry gate. Walk beyond this to the road where a left turn takes you back to the start of the walk.

--------------------<{}>--------------------

My body is a temple – but nobody worships there.

Walk 12: Brierley

Beavers to the rescue!

A pleasant walk almost entirely through woodland exploring some of Dean's industrial remains, before returning through a rarely visited woodland gorge. One or two short climbs but paths are good throughout.

Distance	6 miles (10 km)
Route	Brierley – Serridge Inclosure – Greathough Brook
Maps	OS Explorer Map OL14, and OS Landranger 162
Getting there	The walk starts near Brierley which lies on the A4136 road.
Start/Parking	There are two minor roads that leave the north side of the A4136 at Brierley. Take the road signposted 'The Pludds' and follow it down through the trees for about a quarter mile until you reach a forestry track on your left. Park near the forestry gate
OS Grid Ref/Postcode	SO621154 / GL17 9DL

Brierley

The village was once a hive of industrial activity with a sawmill and the nearby Trafalgar Pit, which provided employment to many in the community.

The village's industrial upbringing influenced perhaps its most famous resident, the author Winifred Foley. The daughter of a miner, Winifred was born in 1914 and went on to write her autobiographical best seller *A Child in the Forest*, a charming, vibrant and gritty account of her upbringing in the 1920s. Her love of the Forest was never more apparent than in this poignant last paragraph of her opening chapter: "As I dozed off to sleep in the warm safety of our shared bed, I listened to the plaintive wind in the forest trees which seemed to me to be the sighs of all the people that had died in our village, who wanted to come back to the forest instead of going to heaven".

This walk sets off for the nearby pit along a route that could easily have been used by the men of Winifred's family for generations.

The walk

Return to the road junction at Brierley along the minor road which, because of the absence of a pavement, has to be negotiated with care. Turn right at the main road and head up the hill passing an old telephone box before reaching a petrol station.

Opposite the petrol station, take a metalled forestry track which leads into the woodland. After about 250m take a right turn and continue past a forestry barrier. This broad path passes through some mixed woodland before bearing left as a power line joins from the right. The line is supported on metal towers at first but after a short distance these give way to poles.

At the first pole a path drops away through the undergrowth to the right leading to a pond about 50 metres away; this is well worth a visit for the water lilies which occur naturally here. They play a vital role in reducing the amount of algae in the pond by shading the surface and excluding light, their leaves also providing a hiding place for Carp. Beautiful though their blooms are, they are short lived, typically lasting only three or four days

Walk in the Wye Valley and Forest of Dean

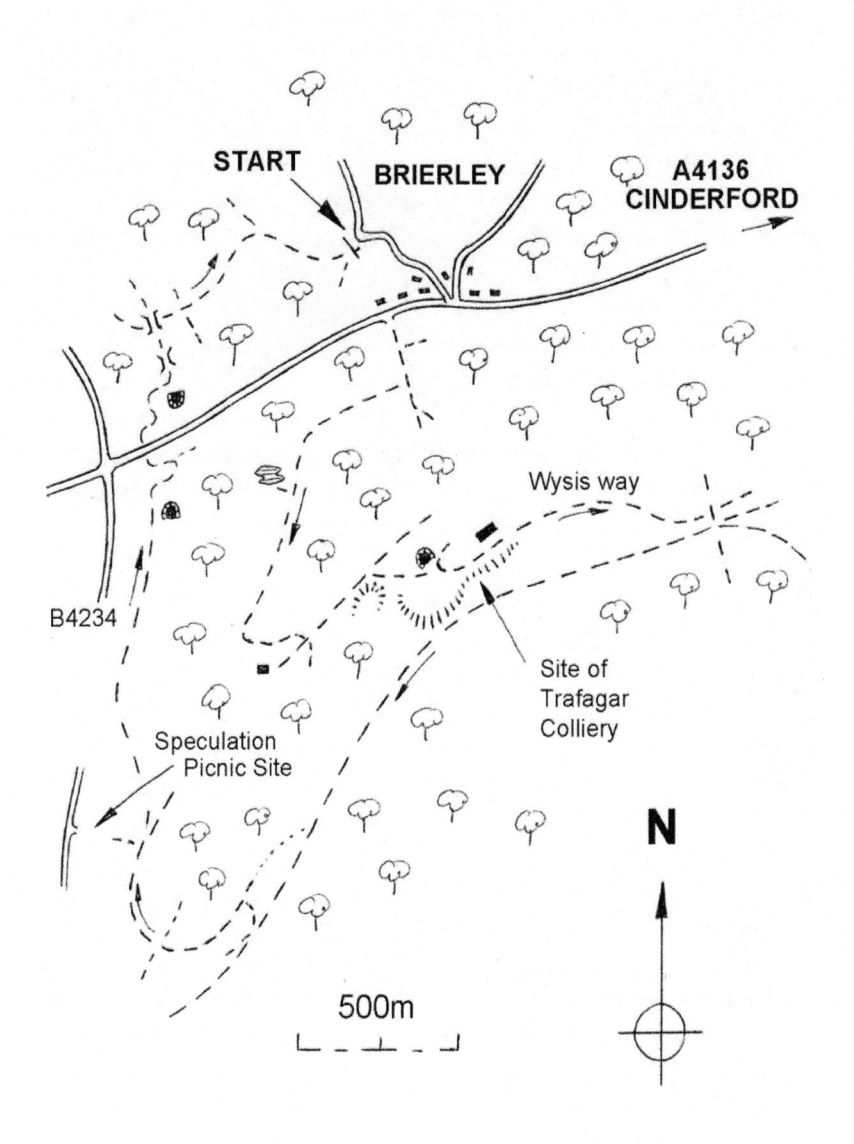

Return to the path by the same route and continue through the woodland. Just before the fourth pole the track bends right but you must continue straight on up towards the fifth pole where you turn left. Follow the path as it climbs steeply through the beech trees until you reach a forestry track. Turn left here and, after passing through a forestry gate, continue in an easterly direction along a high ridge which passes through some delightful stands of beech trees.

Shortly a pine cloaked hill rises abruptly on your right. This was the spoil tip of the Trafalgar Colliery and, as soon as it drops away again, turn right onto a path which skirts the edge of the waste tip. This is the Wysis way and you follow this gently downhill into the old colliery. At the bottom of the hill, just before you reach a track, pause for a moment and look to your left.

About 50m away, in a small abandoned quarry, a disused tramway tunnel may be seen, though in summer it may be necessary to venture away from the path in order to see it clearly. This 150 metre long tunnel connected the colliery to the 'Strip-and-at-it' mine on the other side of the ridge. Many of the Forest mines had colourful names – 'Catch can', 'As you like it', 'Pot lid' and 'Never fear' being examples of others in this area.

Return the way you came and turn right onto a track which swings left to pass a substantial old house.

There are few obvious remains of the colliery now but this house is an exception being built for the owner in Victorian times. Trafalgar Colliery opened in around 1860 and was notable as one of the first in the world to use electric lighting. The hillside here would have echoed to the sound of heavy industry: the rumble of laden wagons on the tramway, the distant thunder of explosives in a quarry, the rattle of coal on a shovel, and the hiss of steam from behind the boiler house door. All is peaceful now but if the breeze is blowing in the right direction you might still hear the whirring of the winding gear at the end of the shift; but maybe not. Nature has been busy here and what remains is hard to find.

The mine was worked quite profitably until 1919 when the electric water pump which had served the company well for over 30 years suddenly failed causing flooding of the lower levels. The pit battled on for a few more years before finally closing in 1925 with reportedly over 2 million tons of coal still to be worked.

Walk beyond the house following the track-bed of a tramway built to serve the colliery.

This tramway was in turn superseded by a railway, the sidings of which occupied the level area down to your right. As you leave the colliery behind look over your left shoulder to see the high retaining walls of the screens. A little further on a short section of fence on the right protects another relic of the mine but its purpose is unclear.

Continue along the path which forms an avenue through the pine trees until you reach a metalled track. Turn right here and right again a little further on at the site of Drybrook Road Station on what was once the Severn and Wye railway. This is now part of a network of cycle trails through the forest. If you're finding the going easy now it's because the gradient here is 1 in 40, very steep by railway standards and noticeable even to us as we bowl along. As the track makes a gentle left turn it passes under what appears to be an arch. Pause here and note how the ground rises steeply to the right.

We have encountered the spoil tips of the Trafalgar Colliery again and, following a serious slip here in 1887, this retaining wall and buttress was built in 1904 to protect the railway.

After walking along a section of embankment you reach a junction of paths. Look over your right-hand shoulder and take a path which climbs steeply uphill. This soon swings left to join the trackbed of a railway.

This was the former track-bed of the Severn and Wye railway's extension to Lydbrook which was opened in 1874. Like all forest lines it was freight which generated the revenue, passenger services being terminated as long ago as 1929. Nowadays this forms part of a network of cycle trails through the forest.

Eventually you pass to the right of Speculation Picnic site where you fork left onto a track signposted 'Branch to Lydbrook 2.5km'. Continue along the former track-bed which soon enters a wide cutting of considerable depth which is shaded by a mixture of oak and beech. The path gradually climbs out of the cutting and an old bridge is visible on the right. Your route here is straight on but take a short detour onto the bridge to glimpse the southern portal of Mirystock Tunnel.

This tunnel is 221 metres in length and took two years to construct, finally opening in 1874.

Return to the path which meanders up through the pines to reach the busy A4136, which must be crossed with care to reach the path on the other side. This path then zig-zags back down to the track-bed again where you turn left to cross a trestle bridge.

If you have a moment to spare turn right instead and take a look at the northern portal of the tunnel seen earlier. It can be seen at the end of a tremendous rock cutting, the best view being obtained by climbing up the left hand embankment. With the trees perched precariously over the tunnel mouth and the steep sides of the cutting, it's no surprise to learn that in 1898 a train was derailed here by a fallen boulder. This historic tunnel had been buried under spoil since the 1970s but was uncovered thanks to the efforts of a group of friends who played here in their childhood. Their campaign to get permission and funding to uncover the historic arch came to a climax in 2006 when they won a grant from the Big Lottery Fund after viewers of ITV's People's Millions voted it to victory. Not content with removing 30,000 tons of spoil they wanted to route the cycle path through the tunnel so that cyclists can avoid the busy road above. Unfortunately, these plans were frustrated by the discovery that the tunnel supports the hibernation of Lesser and Greater Horseshoe Bats which are protected by strict conservation laws. The picture shows the tunnel when first uncovered in 2006 and if you compare this with the present view you can see how quickly nature has reclaimed the area.

Mirystock Tunnel in 2006

Return to the trestle bridge and follow the route of the disused railway which leaps across the pretty Greathough Brook on an embankment, giving us a delightful airy walk through the tree canopy. Immediately in front of a second trestle bridge, look for a gap in the fence on the right and take a path that falls steeply down to an old tramway. Turn right onto this and follow the path to another junction where you continue straight on, keeping to the left of a fence.

Greathough Brook has much to do, falling around 200m on its 4km journey to the Wye at Lydbrook. In its haste it has eroded a narrow gorge here and, as it gurgles away innocently on your right, you might be amazed at what it has been guilty of when in full spate. Lydbrook has been subjected to several devastating floods. In 2012 a major flood saw over 4 feet of water inundate the centre of the village, prompting the council to spend £290,000 on new flood defences.
This fence has been erected to create a six-acre site for the introduction of beavers into the Forest of Dean. Beavers create ponds pools and ditches which form ideal habitats for various species of insects birds and small mammals. It is also hoped that their structures will slow the descent of water through Greathough Brook, and alleviate the risk of flash flooding. Possibly an environmentally beneficial and cost-effective solution to an old problem!

Eventually the path joins a forestry track. Bear right and follow the fence up this lonely valley until the track returns you to your starting point.

--------------------<{}>--------------------

One of the great certainties of life, along with death, taxes and Coronation Street, is that if you park in an empty car-park, the next person to arrive will park right next to you.

Walk 13: Speech House
A bitter rivalry

A walk in the heart of the forest along a route entirely in woodland visiting three ponds and an extensive viewpoint. Some careful navigation is required for the first mile after which the route follows part of the cycle trail which is clearly way-marked. One short hill but paths are good throughout.

Distance	6 miles (9.5 km)
Route	Speech House – Cannop – New Fancy
Maps	OS Explorer Map OL14, and OS Landranger 162
Getting there	The walk starts near Speech House which stands on the B4226 west of Cinderford
Start/Parking	Head for the Cyril Hart Arboretum Picnic site. Leave the B4226 at Speech House and turn south onto a road signposted Parkend, Yorkley and Blakeney. Continue along this for about 300m until the entrance to the picnic site can be seen on the left. Follow the road into the picnic area and park under the oak trees. This is not to be confused with the entrance to the Arboretum which lies to the east of Speech House on the main road
OS Grid Ref/Postcode	SO622118 / GL16 7EL

What are the saddest words you could possibly read?
While you're thinking about this I'll give you mine: 'Dismantled Rly'. This provokes an evocative image of a little steam engine propelling a (nearly empty) carriage along a branch line embankment in front of a setting sun. A time long gone by. There's nothing sad about the dismantled railways in the Forest of Dean now that they have nearly all been converted to cycle routes. The principal cycle route in the Forest was once the Severn and Wye Railway Loop Line which returns the unwitting cyclist back to the point they started from. This unique route is a legacy of a bitter battle between two railway companies which, had the outcome been different, would have meant a far less convenient outcome for the unsuspecting cyclist.

It's also a delightful walking route, and this walk explores some of the industrial sites to be seen along the way.

The Walk
From the picnic site, walk back up to the road and turn right to follow the road until it makes a junction with the B4226 at Speech House.

The Speech House Hotel was originally built in 1676 as a hunting lodge for Charles II, and was soon recognised as the administrative centre of the Forest of Dean. The King appointed judicial officers, known as Verderers, who dealt with offences such as the taking of venison, the illegal removal or destruction of woodland, and encroachment through unauthorised enclosure and building. The largest room became the Verderers court where the accused would make a 'speech' in their defence. By the 18th century offences were dealt with in the magistrates courts by justices of the Peace, rather than in the Verderers Court, although the Verderers retained the power of enquiry into encroachment. These powers resulted in hundreds of convictions,

Walk in the Wye Valley and Forest of Dean

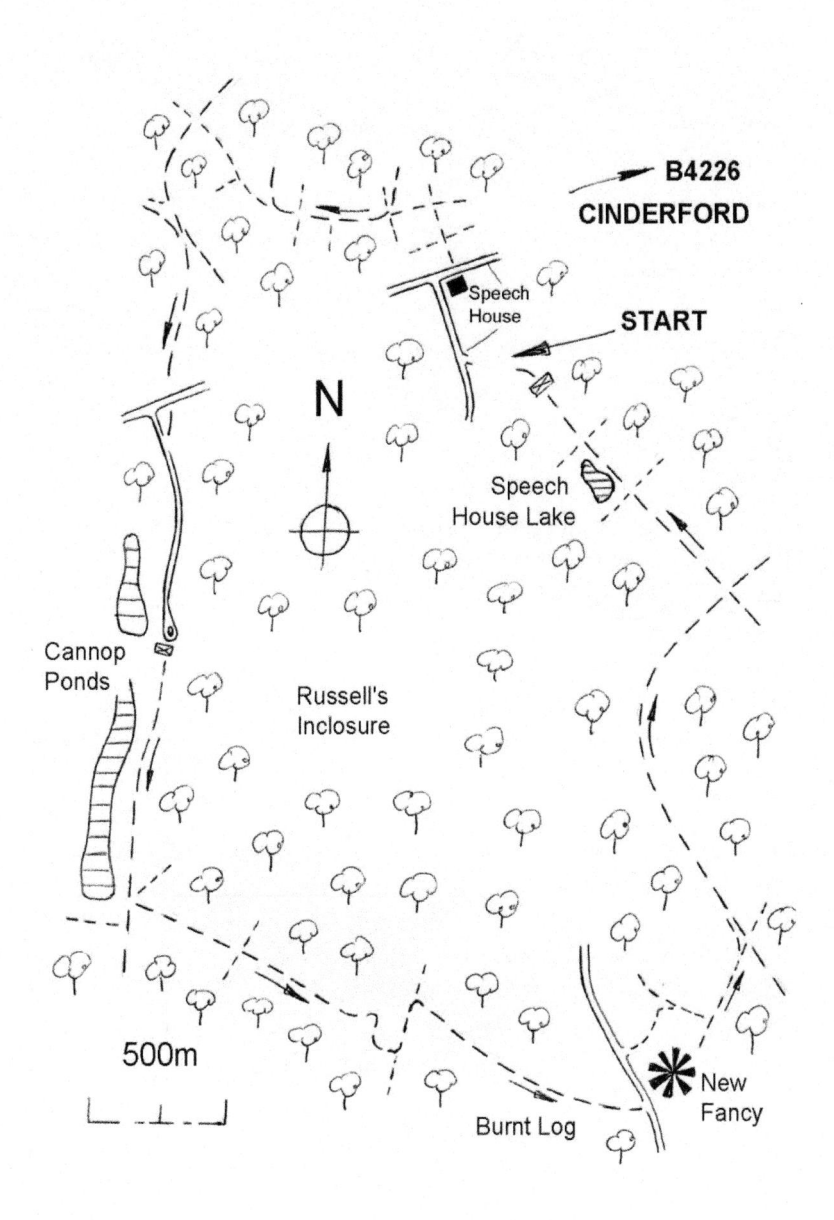

Speech House

-mainly for the unauthorised opening of quarries and the building of houses.

Today their role is largely ceremonial, although they can still impose the death penalty for deer poaching. However, they are only authorised to carry out this sentence on the gibbet outside the hotel. The gibbet, however, has been mislaid, therefore no gibbet – no hanging!

The Speech House is now a lovely 37 bedroom hotel, which boasts two 7ft by 7ft four poster beds. A number of bedrooms are named after trees, and most of them look out into the canopy of the forest's 20 million trees.

Turn right at the junction, and cross the road outside the front of the building, looking for a way-mark post to the left of a pillar which marks the centre of the forest. Leave the road here, and walk down a broad grassy area for about 75m until you reach a path at the bottom. Go straight on here, passing through a gate near a way-mark post and descend steeply through some conifers. At the next junction of paths turn left, and follow this path through the trees.

Shortly you arrive at a section of brick pavement which is part of the 'Sculpture Trail' which starts from nearby Beechenhurst Lodge, a local picnic and amenity site. Since 1983 artists have been commissioned to provide artworks at various points along the route and this is an example. The words are from a German folk song and link the local forest with a similar one in northern Germany, the home of the artist.

Paths exit to the left and right at regular intervals over the next few hundred metres, but you must continue straight on through all of them. Eventually you find yourself on a forestry track which soon begins to descend through the woodland. After going straight on at a junction of paths governed by a waymark post, the track begins to swing to the right.

Leave the track here and continue straight on using a path that drops down through the trees to reach the embankment of an old railway line. Turn left onto this and walk along this well engineered path through the woodland.

This was formerly the course of the Severn & Wye Railway line which was opened in 1868 to serve the many collieries in the area. Traffic peaked just before the First World War, when up to 13 trains a day used the line; but this had dropped to one a day by 1932, and in the 1950s this section of line was closed. This is part of a cycle trail so look out for cyclists.

After making a gradual left turn, a path climbs away to the left.
This was once a short branch line serving the former Speech House Colliery – now the site of Beechenhurst Lodge.

Continue straight on and, within a few metres, another old branch line heads away over your shoulder to the right. This now leads to a nearby cycle hire centre, but once served Cannop Colliery – now the site of a highways depot.
The track now reaches the busy B4226. Cross this with care to re-join the track on the other side.
This was the site of Speech House Road Station but virtually nothing remains now. Continue ahead to join the metalled road which leads towards the picnic area at Cannop Ponds. The low brick wall to your right marks the course of another branch line serving a wood distillation works. This road is used by motorists heading for the picnic area so please exercise caution.

As you approach the picnic area the road splits in two. Take the right hand fork to reach a gate on the far side. Pass through the gate, and follow the track beyond which passes to the left of a second pond. At the end of this pond look out for a number of paths that leave the cycle track on the left near a way-mark post.
This is Cannop Wharf where stone and coal arrived by tramway from nearby Bixslade for transportation south to Lydney.

Speech House

You need to turn left here, ignoring the sharp left turn that climbs up to a gate in favour of a second left turn popular with cyclists. For the moment though, walk a few metres further on to find a right turn which leads you to Cannop Pond.

This path follows the route of the Bixslade tramway which originally crossed the Cannop valley on an embankment. The Forest of Dean Iron Company built a dam against the embankment in 1825 to create Cannop Pond; the water being used to drive their waterwheel in Parkend. Although the iron works were dismantled in 1908 the pond remains as an attractive scenic legacy and is a delightful place to watch the many different species of wildfowl which make their home here.

Return to the point mentioned earlier and follow this arrow-straight cycle-path for a kilometer after which it zig zags steeply up to a forestry track. Turn left here and, within a few metres, take the next right to stay with the cycle track as it climbs up the hill.

Shortly the track levels out and away to the left, cloaked in conifers, can be seen the second of the two spoil tips associated with the former New Fancy colliery. After passing through a gate, signposted 'Burnt Log', walk up to a road and turn left. Follow this road for about 150m and then take a right turn into the New Fancy picnic spot, named after the colliery that once occupied the site. After a short distance two separate car parks can be seen, one to your left and another to your right.

Your route takes a path which leaves the far end of the left hand car park but, for the moment, turn into the right hand car park and look for a path which climbs away to the right. This follows the rim of the collieries' original spoil tip to reach a commanding viewpoint.

The colliery opened in 1832 and closed in 1944 after 3.5 million tons of coal had been extracted. Over this period about

750,000 tons of shale and other waste were brought from the pithead and dumped here to form a vast flat topped spoil tip which became a prominent local landmark. In 1961 two thirds of the top was removed and used for the foundations of Llanwern Steel works in South Wales; the rest being landscaped in 1975 to form this car park, picnic site and viewpoint.

Retrace your steps, and look for a path that leaves the far end of the left-hand car park. This descends through the trees for about 100m until another path joins from the left near a cycle track finger post. Your route is straight on here, but for the moment turn sharp left onto this path which takes you along the route of an old railway siding that reached the colliery from the nearby main line.

Shortly, you reach the high walls of the colliery screens, where the coal was screened (sorted) by size prior to loading onto trucks. The sidings here were built on a slight gradient so the trucks could be manoeuvred as they ran under their own weight.
In Victorian times, two railway companies competed for the traffic from this lucrative pit. The Forest of Dean Central Railway reached it first from Blakeney along the valley of the Blackpool Brook with high hopes of continuing straight across the Forest towards Wales. The rival Severn & Wye Railway had already submitted plans for their own line which reached out from Lydney along the Cannop Valley before looping back round through the Forest. The Central had led a troubled existence; traffic had not lived up to expectations, and it now faced the loss of its main source of revenue to its rival, who had the advantage of shipping facilities at Lydney. The resulting conflict was only resolved in front of a House of Lords select committee who ruled in favour of the S&W. The Central never recovered and, by 1877, were so impoverished that they lacked sufficient funds even to cover the small expense involved in publishing their annual accounts!

Speech House

A resident of Cannop Ponds

Go back the way you came and go straight ahead at the junction of paths you left a few moments ago. Continue along the trackbed of the old siding, and pass through a gate to reach a junction of paths near a cycle track finger post. Turn left here and follow this track for about 350m until it makes a left turn. Go straight on here for a few metres up a slight rise to reach the track bed of an old railway line. You are now back on the course of the old Severn & Wye railway which you left behind at Cannop Pond. Turn left onto the old line which eventually curves right to cross two railway bridges.

The first carried the old line over the Blackpool Brook and the second– aptly named 'Central Bridge' – carried the S&W over its deadly rival, the Central, which abandoned the route below you without even completing it. The Central's ultimate aim was to reach a colliery north of here which promised substantial traffic for the new railway but the mine never reached production due to flooding – literally a tempting bait on the end of the line!

About 400m beyond this bridge, a signpost heralds your arrival at 'Spruce Ride', a broad tree-lined avenue which crosses the cycle track at this point. You turn left onto this and bid farewell to the old railway line as it begins its 7km loop back round to where you first met it near the start of the walk. Follow this magnificent tree lined avenue through the conifers until you reach a crossroads of tracks at the bottom of a dip in the track. Your route is straight on.

Take a few minutes to explore Speech House Lake, which is reached by turning left at this crossroads. The lake was formed by the damming of Blackpool Brook to form a nature reserve.

Return to your route, and continue along Spruce Ride until you reach a gate. Pass through this gate to reach the start of the walk.

Walk 14: Darkhill and Bixslade

A brave daughter saves her family from ruin

This walk, predominantly through woodland and exploring some of Dean's industrial archaeology, makes a gentle climb to Coalway following the track-bed of a disused railway through some wonderful deciduous woodland. From there, the route makes a steady descent down a wooded valley along the course of an old tramway. There are one or two muddy spots but, in the main, the route follows well-established paths and trails.

Note that the route passes near old mines and quarry faces which can be dangerous. Please exercise due care and do not venture underground.

Distance	6 miles (9.5 km)
Route	Nagshead Nature Reserve – Milkwall – Coalway – Bixslade
Maps	OS Explorer Map OL14, and OS Landranger 162
Getting there	The walk starts at the south end of Cannop Ponds on the B4234
Start/Parking	Park at a lay-by on the west side of the B4234 immediately south of Cannop Ponds. A power line crosses the road at this point and there is another lay-by on the east side by a stone works
OS Grid Ref/Postcode	SO607099 / GL15 4JS

The Walk
At the north end of the lay-by take a forest track that leaves the road in a westerly direction. After about 100m, as the track bends right, take a footpath off to the left. This is the route of the former Bixslade Tramway which soon reaches another a forestry track. Turn left here, ignoring the old tramway which continues straight on (you will be returning by this route later). As the track begins a right hand turn, look left for a forestry barrier. Continue beyond the barrier into the Hagshead Nature Reserve.

These trees are over 200 years old and constitute one of the best tracts of broadleaved woodland in the district. This is the 750 acre RSPB Nagshead Nature Reserve, which is a significant site for hawfinches, pied flycatchers, redstarts, and other woodland birds. All three species of native woodpecker can be found in these woods, and overhead you may be lucky enough to see buzzards and sparrow-hawks.

After a short initial climb, the gradient eases a bit until the path levels out near a nature trail that climbs off to the right. Ignore this, and continue along the broad path which soon begins a gradual descent through the woodland.

Eventually, a path tempts you down to the left, but you must continue straight on until you reach a forestry road which sweeps around in a long curve in front of you. Across the road, directly ahead of you, is a five-bar gate adjacent to a marker post. This is your route, but you may want to continue a short way along the forestry road to your left to reach the RSPB Information Centre.

The Information Centre has toilet facilities and is open 10 am until 4 pm at weekends between the Easter and August bank holidays.

Return to the five-bar gate and pass through it to make a gentle descent through woodland accompanied by the gurgling Black Spell Brook, which lies hidden in a gully down to your left.

Darkhill and Bixslade

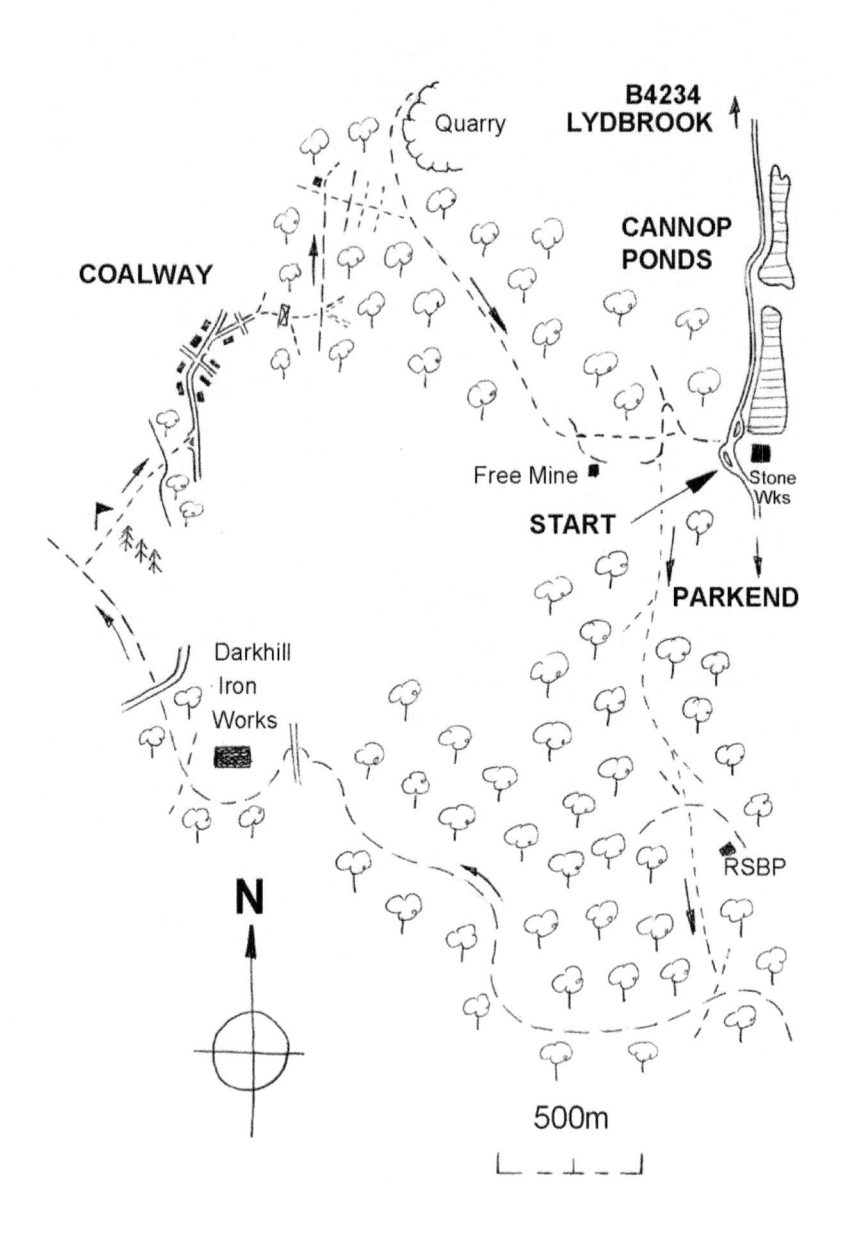

At the bottom of the hill, immediately beyond a forestry barrier, turn right onto a metalled track which passes to the right of a cottage. Within a few metres, turn sharp right at a crossroads, taking a well-made path which passes between two boulders.

This route is now a cycle track but was formerly the Parkend to Coleford railway line, which climbed for most of its length at a gradient of 1 in 30. While this affords us an almost unnoticed climb up the valley, this steep and sinuous route created operating difficulties for the railway. Goods trains were restricted to 8 wagons, the two engines needed for this load being required to push rather than pull their train up the gradient to guard against runaway wagons.

Nature has re-claimed this narrow wooded valley and it's hard now to imagine the extent to which this area once echoed to the sound of heavy industry. The rumbling of wagons on a tramway, the distant thunder of explosives in a quarry, the dust and the various spoil-tips all contributed to a scene quite different from what you see today. After a while you arrive at Point Quarry, where an old tramway passes underneath the route using a tunnel, the abutments of which can be seen down on the left hand side.

Eventually the path reaches the Coalway Road. The old railway bridge has been dismantled here, so the path detours alongside the road to cross it on the level. Pick up the path on the other side of the road. Shortly, a path climbs away to the right – ignore this, and follow the path as it drops to the left.

Your route now takes you past the remains of David Mushet's Titanic Iron Works at Darkhill which was built in 1819. Pause by the information board, which is well placed to provide the best view across the sprawling ruins. For years the railways had been experiencing problems with the brittleness of the iron rail in use at the time and, in 1857, David's son Robert developed a steel alternative. This was first tested at Derby station and the

Darkhill and Bixslade

improvement was dramatic. Life expectancy of the rail was now measured in decades rather than months and Mushet's steel rail was installed all over the country.

While Henry Bessemer is credited with the development of the steel making process it was the pioneering work of Mushet here at Darkhill which perfected Bessemer's process. Further experiments with tungsten, chrome, magnesium and titanium alloys helped end the iron age and usher in the new age of steel. While Bessemer patented the process and became a wealthy man, Mushet never fully capitalised on the commercial possibilities of his steel alloys and it was left to others to develop them for world-wide use in everything from drill bits to turbine blades.

By 1866 Mushet found himself in ill health and facing ruin. Unbeknown to him, his sixteen year old daughter Mary, grimly determined, made the long journey to Bessemer's London office. Perched on the edge of her chair, she leaned across the great man's desk and confronted Bessemer, claiming that his success was based on her father's discoveries. The formidable steel magnate challenged the young girl to take her case to the high court but Mary, undeterred, replied that although they lacked the money to do so there was nevertheless a strong moral obligation. Whatever Bessemer's motives were, he was sufficiently moved to immediately write out a cheque sufficient to pay off the family debts and safeguard her father's home. This would have been a bold move for a young girl at the end of the 20th Century but was nothing short of breathtaking in the 19th, considering the difficulties of travel and the customs and etiquette of the day.

Leave Darkhill by continuing along the old railway which is soon crossed by a track near a conservation area. Follow the old railway line as it bends to the right until eventually the path leaves the now overgrown track-bed to continue alongside it. There are a number of paths off to the left, but continue straight on along the left-hand side of the old line which now occupies a shallow cutting. As you approach a mobile home park on your right, the path dog-legs back onto the course of the old line and narrows as it approaches a road. Cross the road where a metallic sign proudly announces the start of the Milkwall to Coleford section of the cycleway.

Operational free mine

The path is metalled from now on and benefits from some modest landscaping as it passes through the village. Milkwall, and its neighbour Coalway, are typical forest villages having established themselves in a rather haphazard fashion around mine workings now long since abandoned.

Within a few hundred metres, the well-tended fairway of a golf course can be seen through the hedge on your right and, shortly afterwards, a footpath fingerpost directs you up onto it. Leave the cycle track here by way of a small flight of steps and strike out across the golf course in a north easterly direction, aiming for a point just to the left of a line of conifers. Maintain your bearing beyond the conifers and cross a couple of fairways. In the distance

Darkhill and Bixslade

a line of trees and shrubs mark the boundary of the golf course. A dog-leg in this boundary to your right brings these trees and shrubs closer to you. Maintain your straight line and follow the boundary of the course round to the left where a path leaves the course between a white house and the sixteenth tee. After a short walk through some trees you reach a stile next to a finger-post. Cross this stile and walk to the left of a line of cottages before reaching a road about 50m away.

Turn left onto the road and head north into the centre of Coalway until you reach a crossroads passing, on your way, the locally renowned Gibson's Forest Trading Post.

After your sojourn in the woods you could be forgiven for expecting to see a few mules tied to a veranda here, their owners busy inside trading furs, skins and lamp oil, but behind Gibson's modest exterior lies a veritable emporium selling everything for the home and garden.

Continue across the road junction (signposted Broadwell and Milend) and within 100m take the second right onto Old Road, following this until you reach a minor crossroads. Go straight on here and continue to the end of the road where you fork right in front of some trees. Within a few metres you pass through a gate and fork left into the woodland. After about 150m turn left at a junction of paths under a power line. Follow this forestry track to a junction of paths in front of a sub-station. Turn right and walk down through the Beech trees crossing in quick succession a forestry track and two further paths. Continue to follow the power line downhill until, at the bottom, you turn left then right onto the course of the Bixslade Tramway.

This is your route down, but if time allows turn left and walk uphill for a few hundred metres to the far side of a quarry, last used in the 1960s. The path climbs through stands of silver birch to reach a clearing on the far side.

Mature trees have already colonised the quarry floor beneath you and your vantage point allows you to appreciate the sheer scale of this man made pit. The sandstone quarried here was of high quality being used throughout the country in the 19th century to build numerous civic and municipal buildings. Locally it has been used to build Gloucester's Shire Hall and Telford's elegant bridge across the Severn at Over.

Retrace your steps back to the route where soon you are joined by a power line which accompanies you all the way down the valley.

You are now on the route of the old Bixslade tramway which was built in Napoleonic times to transport stone from the quarry and was in regular use until as recently as 1941. At regular intervals, stone sleepers may be seen beneath your feet and some may well display the characteristic holes used to secure the rails to the sleepers. Apart from the stone traffic the tramway served over a dozen mines at various times in its history and most of these lie close to the tramway route. If you are interested in finding some of them, keep an eye on the power line which briefly switches to the left of the path after about 750m.

When the line returns to the right hand side of the path, start counting its supporting poles. About 25m in front of the third pole a fenced off ventilation shaft can be seen adjacent to the path. At the same spot a short path leads off to the right to a gated mine entrance. About 25m beyond the pole, another fenced off shaft can be seen adjacent to the path on the right.

About two-thirds of the way down, you reach a broad forestry track which sweeps across the old tramway to reach a quarry on the left. Your route is straight on here but if time allows head off to the right here and follow this broad track as it makes a brief climb into the trees.

Within a short distance, on the right, is a memorial to the Union Pit mine disaster of 1902 which trapped 7 miners underground. After a rescue attempt lasting 5 days only three of the seven were found alive. The Dean Heritage Museum near Soudley has a contemporary photograph of the rescue effort.

A few metres further on can be seen a working 'free mine', one of only two now remaining in the forest (see walk 19), which maintains a tradition dating back over 700 years. In the 14th century local men won a battle for King Edward I by tunnelling under the fortifications at Berwick upon Tweed, the grateful monarch responding by giving them the right in perpetuity to mine coal in the forest 'without tax or hindrance'.

Return to the tramway and continue downhill. Stay with it across a forestry track and eventually it will return you to the lay-by and the start of the walk.

If time allows cross the road and take a path to the left of the stone works, now the last of its kind in the forest. Most of the works are visible from outside the fence and on a weekday you can see the stone being processed into dressed blocks highly prized for its colour and durability. The water race at the far end is a delightful place to watch the many different species of wildfowl which make their home here.

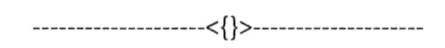

--------------------<{}>--------------------

I still wear 30-waist trousers – I just don't pull them up so far.

Walk 15: Parkend
Black gold

This walk, predominantly through woodland and exploring some of Parkends' industrial archaeology, makes a gentle climb to a charming old miners pub situated in a forest clearing. From there, the route makes a steady descent down a rarely visited wooded valley along the course of an old railway before returning via a local church.

The route follows long established old trails which are good throughout.

Distance	4 miles (6.5 km)
Route	Parkend – Moseley Green
Maps	OS Explorer Map OL14, and OS Landranger 162
Getting there	The walk starts from Parkend which is 4 miles north of Lydney on the B4234
Start/Parking	Head for the crossroads near the restored railway station and then take the road to Coleford. Park just beyond the Fountain Inn on the roadside verge
OS Grid Reference	SO614079 / GL15 4JD

Parkend

In Victorian times Parkend was an important industrial centre but, apart from the station, the only obvious survivor from these times is the imposing four storey field study centre which was originally the engine house of the local iron works. This is now

Parkend

one of Parkends' listed buildings and was part of a complex that included a coke blast furnace, several coal mines and a 51ft waterwheel which remained in service long after steam engines had taken over elsewhere. At the time, this wheel was one of the largest in the country and was driven using water from the Cannop pond further up the valley. Within a mile of the east side of the village, almost 20 coal mines existed at various times during the 19th century, being served by a network of tramways and railways. They had typically colourful names like 'As you like it' and 'Catch Can', but by far the largest were the Royal and Castlemain collieries which lie just outside the village.

In its heyday Parkend was an important railway junction, but it was always freight that generated the revenue, passenger services terminating as long ago as 1929. BR closed the line north of Parkend in the late sixties, but continued to use a branch line alongside the Fountain Inn for a few years to transport ballast from nearby Whitecliffe Quarry. Final closure came in the early 1980s, but a preservation society, the Dean Forest Railway, was already well established and ready to reverse the long years of decline. Initial effort was concentrated on the line between Lydney and their headquarters at Norchard, the station here at Parkend not formally opening until 2006.

Much of the present day village resulted from this industrialisation, only a few cottages existing before 1850. Nowadays only an occasional steam train can wake Parkend from its slumber, the ruins of its coal mines having long since been reclaimed by nature. Its railways are now pleasant walkways and this route explores some of these.

The walk
Walk to the left of the Fountain Inn and head for the Railway Station. After crossing the road, pass through the level crossing and follow the road uphill away from the village.

Shortly on the left you pass Castlemain Mill, now a private house but formerly the offices of the Castlemain Colliery. Further up the hill, on the left behind a bench, lie the brick foundations of the colliery's pumping house.

Follow the road up the hill until, opposite the primary school, you turn left onto a path which heads past some bungalows before climbing through the trees to reach a forest track.
Turn left here and continue down to a T-junction where you can pause for a moment.

The little hill ahead of you, cloaked in conifers, is the spoil tip of the Parkend Royal Colliery, while to your left is a Forestry Commission depot which was built on the site of the colliery. Also on the left, hiding amongst the ferns, are two storage ponds for the colliery pumping engine. Both collieries closed in the 1920's.

Turn right at this T-junction and begin a climb up through the trees. Your route then climbs to the right, escorted through the conifers by a delightful mixture of lime, oak, beech and chestnut. After about 500m the path levels out near a crossroads of paths beside an old oak tree. Continue straight on here, following the track down past a forestry barrier to a road. Turn right and walk along the road for 250m until you reach a road junction. Turn right here onto a forestry track, looking immediately left for a path which heads into the woods. Follow this delightful stretch of path for about 400m through a wooded glade shaded by beech and oak, until you drop steeply down to a crossroads of paths. Over to the left, almost hidden in the undergrowth, lies a fenced off mine shaft and pond – one of many in the vicinity. After turning right at this junction, ignore another path which forks right and plunge into the darkness of the conifers, keeping to the right of a shallow cutting which marks the route of an old tramway.

Shortly you emerge out of the shadows to find yourself walking to the right of the Rising Sun Inn which was built in the early 19th century to serve the local mining community. There were as many as ten mineshafts within a kilometre radius of the Inn, together with associated spoilt tips and tramways but, with their disappearance into the undergrowth, the pub now enjoys an enviable position alone in its forest clearing. It still retains its traditional atmosphere, and its duck pond and grassy areas make it a popular place for families, cyclists and walkers.

Leave the pub along the route of the old tramway, which keeps to the left of the duck pond before entering a stand of conifers. Go straight on across another path until you reach a T- junction between two spoil tips. Turn right here, and follow another old tramway which passes to the right of some mine remains before reaching a road. Cross the road and pick up the route of the old tramway on the other side. You now have an easy amble of about 750m before a path appears on the left just as the track makes a sinewy 'S' bend.

Turn left onto this path and follow it down into a wooded valley. Further down a wide track crosses your path but continue on down until, just before you reach the brook at the bottom of the valley, the path is crossed by a straight and level path on top of an embankment. Turn right onto this, and walk along this embankment, which follows the route of the former Severn & Wye railway line.

When built in 1872, the Severn & Wye railway line provided a much more efficient outlet for forest coal, iron and stone than the tramways they superseded. This is a beguiling section of the walk, with the high embankment allowing you to walk through the tree canopy to the accompaniment of the bubbling Rudge Brook.

Soon you leave the embankment behind and the trackbed occupies a ledge above the Rudge Brook. About 200m beyond this start looking for a path which climbs up from the left. Turn right opposite this and climb up between the concrete posts of a derelict kissing gate.

Another path immediately crosses in front of you, but go straight on, up through the trees along a path that can be a bit overgrown in summer. After about 50m turn right onto another path which almost immediately climbs up to a broad forestry track. Turn left here, and follow the track for about a kilometre as it winds around the hillside until it eventually starts to go downhill.

As it begins to level out and bend to the right, look out for two paths that head off to the left. Ignore the first, which sneaks up on you from over your left shoulder, in favour of the second, which climbs up through the trees to a forestry barrier.

Follow the metalled track beyond this to pass to the left of the octagonal shaped St Pauls church which dates back to 1822.

Rising Sun Inn

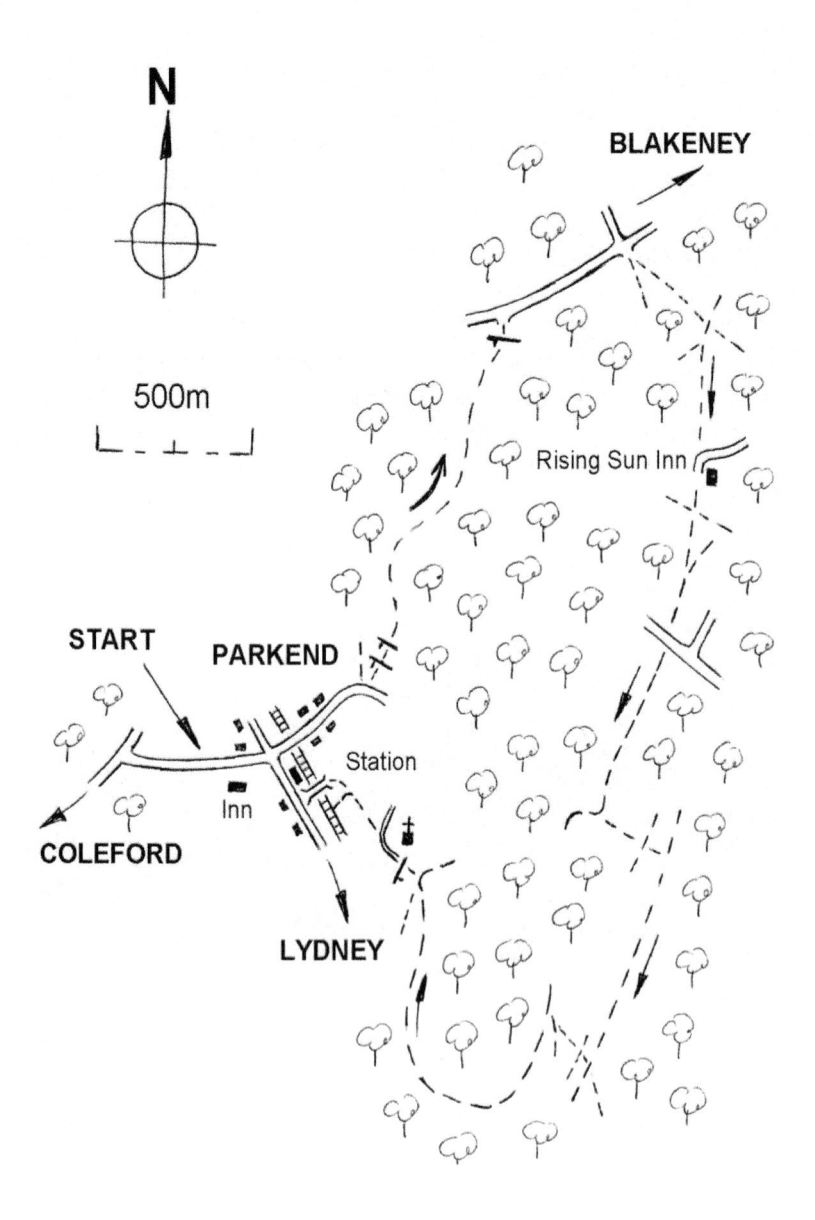

Parkend

As you leave the church behind, look out for a gravel track which leaves the driveway on the left. Follow this down the hill and, when it later bends left, go straight on, heading for a modern detached house in the distance. Eventually, the path narrows and makes a left turn and soon you unexpectedly find yourself on a pedestrian bridge carrying you over the Dean Forest Railway. Cross the bridge and pass through a small gate to reach the road. Turn right here and, before turn left to reach the Fountain Inn, note the rails embedded in the tarmac

At one time, a branch line left the station and crossed the road to pass between the Fountain and the cottages opposite. When the branch was constructed in 1864 it was necessary to raise the road by about 2m between the inn and the cottages in order to make a level run for the train. This meant that the ground floor of the houses on each side of the road became cellars, and their first floors became level with the road.
Another storey was added and new front doors were built. As you approach the cottages, note that the front door has been built on the side of the house, the proximity of the railway precluding access at the front. The striking bay window of the Inn was built on top of the earlier one, now down in the cellar!

Continue on a few metres to the start of the walk

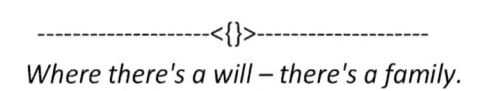

--------------------<{}>--------------------
Where there's a will – there's a family.

Walk 16: Old Park Wood
The Devil's Chapel

An easy walk through old woodland where Buzzards circle overhead. There are one or two steep sections and a couple of places where the directions will need to be followed carefully.

Distance	4 miles (6.5 km)
Route	Upper Old Park Wood – Hollywell Wood – Broom Hill
Maps	OS Explorer Map OL14, and OS Landranger 162
Getting there	The walk starts just south of Bream on the B4231 road.
Start/Parking	Park in a lay-by on the west side of the B4231 about ½ mile south of Bream near a road-side cottage.
OS Grid Ref/Postcode	SO607050 / GL15 6ER

The walk

Follow the main road away from Bream for about 100m, passing some tired roadside cottages, to reach a forestry track which leaves the road on the right. Round the gate, and walk into the woodland. Ignore a track which joins from the left, and continue on towards the Devils Chapel, one of the biggest areas of Roman and medieval ironworking in Dean.

This labyrinth of mysteriously shaped hollows is a naturally occurring geological feature which developed over millions of years. They appear in many of the limestone outcrops around the edge of the Forest, and early man found iron ore in veins and pockets in the exposed rock faces of these amazing landscape features. Man has collected iron here since Roman times, and in places they followed the veins of iron ore deep underground.

Much of the iron ore would have been smelted locally in small furnaces known as bloomeries. The iron ore was heated to a high temperature in the bloomery by the burning of charcoal, which separated enough of the iron from other impurities within the ore to allow it to be made into useful objects.

Most of the Devil's Chapel is visible from your route, which is the only public right of way through this private woodland; but the evidence is that many wander from the path to venture into the winding chasms. Do not linger though – at dusk this can be an un-nerving place; its covering of lush undergrowth creating a mystical atmosphere where you could stumble upon Merlin holding court. The ground is torn open, moss and lichen covered boulders appear to have been randomly thrown about. Trees cling perilously to the top of limestone pillars, their roots reaching over the edges of the rock like the gnarled fingers of an irritated old giant who's mislaid his spectacles. The whole scene looks like something out of Tolkien's Middle Earth; the trees lean towards you, their branches want to wrap themselves around you and draw you in!

To break the spell, look away and continue along the track through the woodland. Where it swings right, take a footpath which leaves the track on the left. Turn right immediately afterwards, passing through a gate to follow a path which winds down through the trees. As you approach the edge of the woodland some way-mark posts direct you around an old lime kiln before taking you to a stile which you cross to reach some open parkland.

Old Park Wood

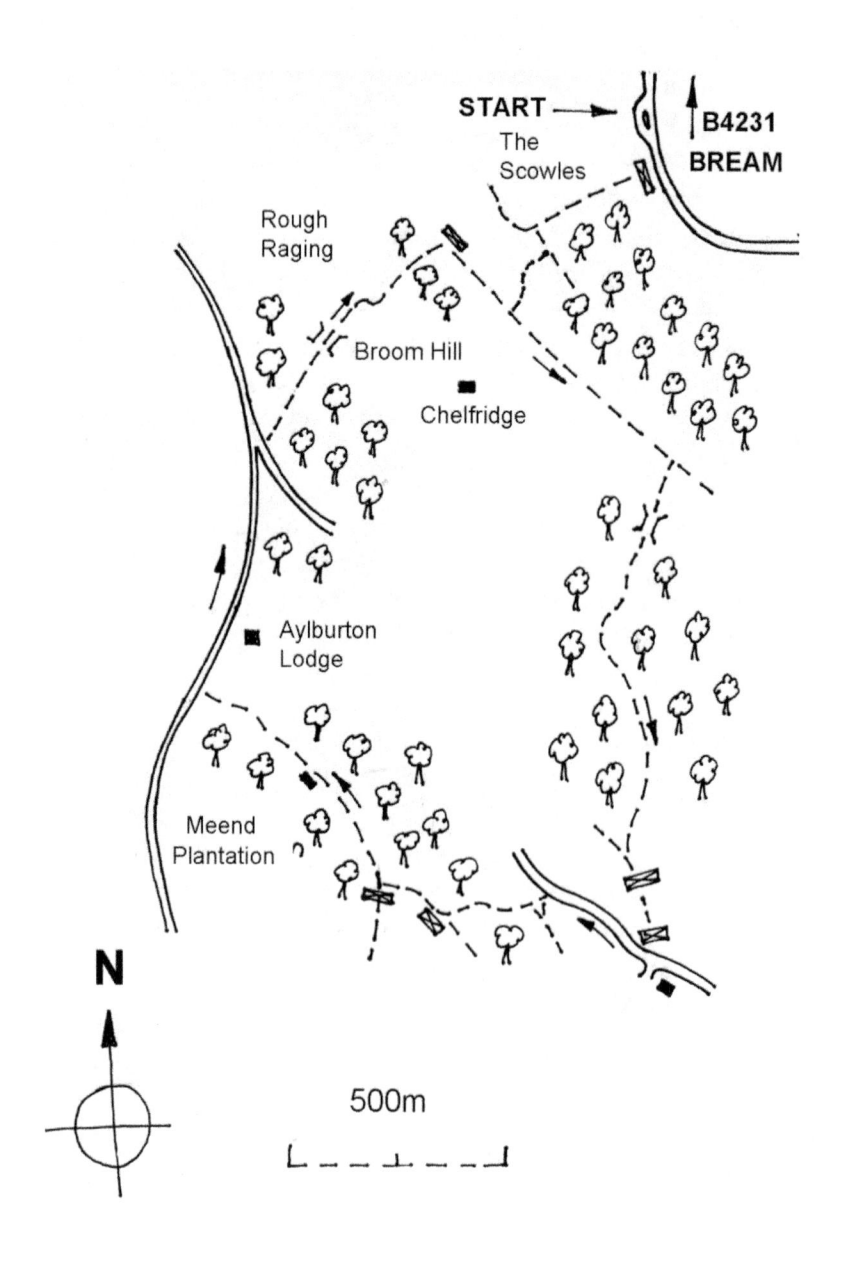

START
The Scowles
B4231
BREAM
Rough Raging
Broom Hill
Chelfridge
Aylburton Lodge
Meend Plantation
N
500m

Opposite you are a couple of farm buildings. Your need to turn left here, but pause for a moment and look right; you will be returning this way later.

This area lies within the Lydney Park Estate. Since 1723 it has been in the hands of the Bathurst Family, but prior to this was granted to Sir William Wintour by Elizabeth I in recognition of his services against the Spanish Armada. His grandson, the ruthless and determined Sir John Wintour, declined to follow the family's naval tradition, and became the second most important iron master in the realm, at one point owning six furnaces and eight forges. It's unlikely that this tree-filled view would have existed in Wintour's time because, in 1634, he was fined the enormous sum of £20,230 for his over-zealous clearing of Crown timber. He backed the wrong side in the Civil War and ended up in the Tower of London. By the time of the Restoration of the Monarchy, in 1660, he had already re-established himself in the area and, by 1663, employed over 500 wood cutters. Perhaps the most lasting testament to this remarkable man is the story of his escape on horseback during the Civil War. After a breathless pursuit by Parliamentary forces, he was chased to the edge of the Wye Gorge just above Chepstow where, to avoid capture, he rode his horse over the cliff that now bears his name (see walk 5).

Resume the walk by strolling downhill for three fields, keeping the woodland on your left. In the third, stay high up close to the fence until you reach a stile in the left hand corner.

Cross the stile and after 50 metres turn right, following a track which falls steeply downhill to cross a footbridge over a stream.

Continue slightly left after this, and follow the track for almost a kilometre until, as you leave the woodland behind, a track joins from the right. Turn left here, and pass through two gates to reach a road where you turn right signposted St Briavels. Follow this road uphill for about 300m until, where the road begins to climb more steeply round a right hand bend, a footpath leaves the road on the left to enter some woodland.

Ignore the path off left and bear right through the trees. Follow this down to the other side of the copse and bear right where a faint path joins from the left. Ignore the farm gate and stile which soon appears on the left, and stay in the trees until you reach an enormous beech tree. Turn right here, ignoring a path down to a stile on the left.

Follow this track uphill for some distance until it narrows before reaching a brick hut. Continue on through the woods and soon a wall joins you on the left. This guides you through the boulder strewn woodland for the next 800m before reaching a stone stile. Further on another wall is negotiated using stone steps built into it. Eventually, after passing to the left of a paddock you reach a road.

Turn right here and follow the road as it climbs uphill for about 600m to reach a junction. Turn sharp right here, signposted Aylburton and Lydney, and look for a path which leaves the road on the left about 10m in front of a telegraph pole.

Follow this path down through the woodland until, just as you begin to feel unsure of the route, you are joined by a wall on the right. Once again, use this wall as a guide and keep to the left of it as the faint path begins to descend more steeply. Eventually it begins to level out near some open pasture on the left where you cross a footbridge over a stream. Still keeping the wall on your right, climb steeply up through some trees until, as you reach the edge of the woodland, a stile is found on the right. Cross this and turn left into a field, to begin a gentler climb up its left hand boundary.

Soon you crest Broom Hill which offers a splendid view down the valley towards the Mansion of Lydney Park, which lies hidden near the Severn Estuary. The garden at Lydney Park is open to the public in the spring and on selected days as part of the National Garden Scheme. It is breathtakingly beautiful, being landscaped into a sheltered wooded valley with pools and dreamy pathways which pass through azaleas and rhododendrons to reach a preserved Roman temple.

Lime kilns near Devil's Chapel

Keeping to the left of the field boundary, drop down through a line of trees before climbing up again to reach a five-bar gate at the entrance to Upper Old Park Wood. Ignore this and turn right, keeping the woodland on your left as you begin a gentle descent through the parkland. On your right are the farm buildings you saw near the start of the walk. Continue across a track leading to the farm and look out for gate on the left. Turn left here and retrace your steps past the old lime kiln and Devil's Chapel until you reach the road. Turn left here and follow the road back to the lay-by.

Walk 17: Wigpool

My own private railway

A walk through woodland to a sublime viewpoint over a remote valley. Return through one of the few remaining areas of heathland in the county. There is one long hill and a few muddy spots but generally the route is along good paths and quiet country lanes.

Distance	6 miles (9.5km)
Route	Mitcheldean Meend – Perlieu Wood – Wigpool Common
Maps	OS Explorer Map OL14, and OS Landranger 162
Getting there	The walk starts at the top of Stenders Hill which lies mid-way between Mitcheldean and Drybrook
Start/Parking	Park in a layby at the top of Stenders Hill. This is reached by climbing away from Drybrook up High Street or from the other end using Mill End, which leaves Mitcheldean near the parish church of St Michael
OS Grid Ref/Postcode	SO655180 / GL17 0JE

The walk
From the lay-by at the top of the hill cross the road and take a track beyond a forestry barrier which heads west into Mitcheldeanmeend Inclosure.

Although now managed by the Forestry Commission, the word 'meend' indicates waste or open ground and is found in many place names in the area.

Paths divert left and right, but continue in a straight line until another barrier is encountered at the far end where the track becomes a road. Ahead of you, on the horizon, can be seen Euroclydon House. Although now a residential home it was originally built in Victorian times as a private dwelling for a wealthy mine owner. Its five-storey tower, complete with wrought iron balcony, was reportedly built so he could keep an eye on his employees at a nearby colliery!

Walk down this road until it reaches a crossroads where you turn left. After about 250m you turn right immediately in front of 'Greystones', a roadside cottage. Walk down the drive and take a path which soon passes between two walls to climb up to a gate. Beyond this, keep the hedgerow on your left for the next six fields while views begin to open up towards the Black Mountains. Ignore a stile in the left hand boundary of the fifth field and press on to the sixth, to reach a stile next to an isolated cottage. After passing the cottage turn right, and follow the enclosed track downhill until it makes a sharp right turn. Go straight on here, passing through a farm gate before climbing up the left hand side of a field.

As you crest the hill, another way-mark post beckons you to the left, but you must continue along the edge of the field passing to the right of a line of oaks. Views open up towards Hope Mansell, while on your right Euroclydon Tower keeps a watchful eye. The path now falls rapidly down to the corner of the field where, after negotiating a stile, a short drive takes you down to a country

Wigpool

lane. Turn left here, and walk down the road as it falls steeply into a valley which can be glimpsed through the roadside beech trees.

Further down, near the bottom of the hill, look out for a bye way on your right. This is your route, but if time allows, stay with the road for a short distance before forking left onto another lane, which climbs to the left of a stand of conifers before reaching a bench on the right-hand side.

Morning mist at Hope Mansell

There may be loftier views of distant hills with rivers that meander lazily into view, but for sheer completeness there can be few more pleasing to the eye than this. The roadless valley appears to be a natural amphitheatre with no obvious exit, but the early morning mist will sometimes reveal the way out, by gathering at the left-hand end like a wisp of cotton wool trying to stop the draught.

Return to the bye-way and follow it along the side of the valley. It passes to the right of some farm buildings and a private house, before climbing gently up a track to reach a road. As you approach the road, a low embankment on the right betrays the presence of a disused railway. As you reach the road, a bridge can be seen which allowed the railway to pass underneath.

This railway was built as a 6 km long extension to an existing line which originally terminated near Drybrook. It was intended to provide an easy outlet for the northern part of the Forest to Ross, Hereford and Wales. Unfortunately, there were problems that delayed its construction and by the time it was completed by the GWR in 1878, an easier and more direct route had been built by the Severn and Wye Railway down the Lydbrook valley, a few kilometres west of here. Faced with this competing route and operating difficulties at the northern end of the line, the GWR never formally opened it for traffic. The only recorded use was made by ganger James of the GWR, who got permission to propel his hand trolley along the line to convey his daughter's luggage through to the station at its northern end, where it made a junction with the Ross to Gloucester Line.

Imagine if you will the squeak, squeak, squeak, of the trolley wheels on the rusty line as ganger James, his arms pumping up and down, rumbled his trolley under the arch of the bridge. He was certainly privileged to be able to use it in this way; costing over one million pounds a mile in today's money, it was surely the most exclusive use ever made of any line in the area! The rails were lifted in 1917, there being no other recorded use of the line in the intervening years save Mr James' little freight delivery.

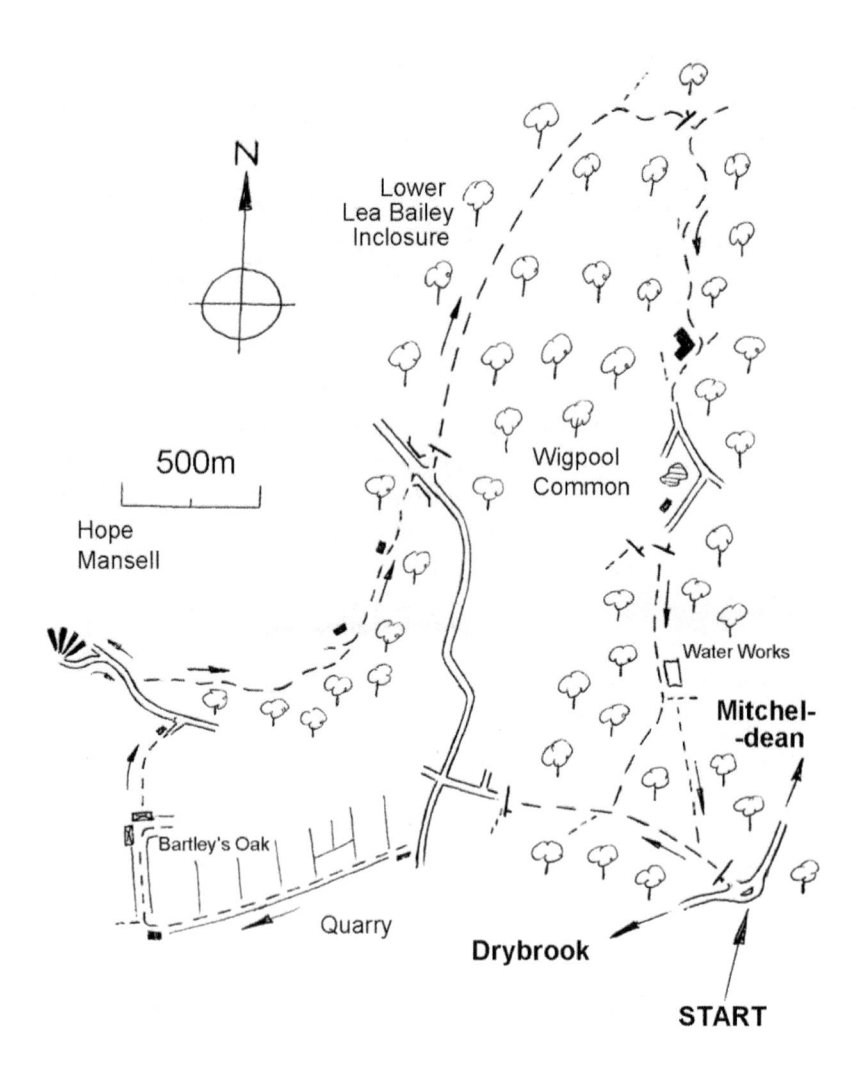

Wigpool

On reaching the road, turn right to cross the bridge and then turn immediately left up a rising forestry track. Walk along this for 1500m until you reach a forestry barrier, after which you turn right, to follow the meandering track up past a number of private drives which tempt you with a break from the steady climb. Finally, the track levels out near a poultry farm where, after ignoring a track which joins from the left, you walk past the sheds to bear left, after which the track becomes a metalled road. Ignore a right fork which soon appears on the right and continue along a dip in the road.

On your right is the Wigpool nature reserve. A remnant of a large area of acidic bog and open heath that once covered the common. The Forestry Commission, in partnership with other conservation bodies, are attempting to restore the area by clearing the alder, willow, birch and gorse. Just before the fork, a faint path leads off to the right to Wigpool itself, one of the few natural ponds in the Forest with records dating back to 1282. Plant species that can be found here include marsh pennywort, lesser spearwort, marsh bedstraw, marsh speedwell, and bog asphodel. The pool is also a good breeding ground for common frogs, and both palmate and smooth newts.

Return to the road and take the right-hand fork which shortly passes to the left of a private house.

This was once the engine house of the Wigpool Iron Mine whose tentacles, both above and below ground, spread all over the common. It was worked between 1861-1883 and, for a short period, around the First World War but, like all mining operations in the Forest, it was necessary to employ a pumping engine to keep the workings free from water. Because the underlying strata in this area is pervious limestone, it was necessary to carry the water away in a man-made trough or 'leat' in order to prevent the water from simply leaking back into the workings. There were two of these, and they extended for some considerable distance across the common.

One headed west towards the old railway bridge you crossed earlier, where briefly the waste water was used in a gold mining operation. The water was used to scour or wash the face of the gold bearing outcrop of quartz conglomerate. The co-ordinates of the gold mine are located elsewhere in this book!

Immediately beyond the old engine house, the road bends to the right, but you must take the first of two forestry tracks that continue almost straight on. As you pass the barrier, the south bound 'leat' is visible as a ditch on your right which eventually leaves the track after a few hundred metres. This track was itself the course of a tramway built to transport the iron ore to a railhead near Cinderford.

Eventually a water treatment works appear on the left, and where its perimeter fence finishes, take a left turn onto a path, immediately looking for a more obvious path on the right. This becomes a broad, well-engineered path, and is the continuation of the tramway through the woods. Under your feet the odd stone sleeper block may still be seen with its characteristic pair of bolt holes. Follow this obvious path through the woodland to emerge at a forestry track where you turn left to walk back to the car.

--------------------<{}>--------------------
The older I get, the better I used to be.

Walk 18: Soudley

A runaway train and other stories!

A truly memorable walk exploring some of the Forest of Dean's industrial past before making a long climb up to a renowned viewpoint. Return via some beautiful woodland ponds. One steep section but paths are good throughout.

Distance	6 miles (9.5 km)
Route	Ruspidge – Soudley – Blaize Bailey – Soudley Ponds
Maps	OS Explorer Map OL14, and OS Landranger 162
Getting there	The walk starts at Ruspidge which is about 2 miles south of Cinderford on the B4227
Start/Parking	Park in Ruspidge on the public road near Tramway Road which joins the main road near an old chapel just north of the New Inn pub
OS Grid Ref/Postcode	SO650117 / GL14 3AR

The walk
Walk a few yards down the main road until, on your left, a stone tablet proudly announces the start of the 'Blue Rock Trail'.

The industrial buildings on the other side of the road belonged to the Eastern United Colliery which closed in 1965.

Leave the road here and follow the trail which occupies the former track-bed of the Forest of Dean Railway, which was built

Soudley

to open up the Forest's rich coal and mineral deposits to ports on the Severn estuary.

After a short distance a trestle bridge carries the path over the Cinderford Brook which is contained in a brick lined trough.

The underlying strata in this part of the valley is pervious limestone and the trough is necessary to minimise the seepage of water into the mine workings beneath.

Further on where the brook switches sides again, there was a siding that led to the now disused Shakemantle Quarry, its sheer vertical faces much prized nowadays by rock climbers. The railway sleepers can still be seen curving away into the trees and embedded in some of them are the original iron bolts.

The path then avoids a disused tunnel by swinging round a rocky outcrop using the route of an old tramway. This is a delightful section of the walk, the brook happily rushing along its man-made course down to your right while you amble along a broad leafy path shaded by mature beech trees. Soon a picnic site is encountered on your right.

Here is a memorial to the children, some as young as eight, who supplemented the family income by working in the narrow mine shafts of the Forest of Dean. There is a carving in blackened oak of a boy hauling boxes of coal ('hods') in the narrow mine shafts – often no more than 60cm high. Much of the heavy hauling was done by the pit ponies which spent their entire working lives underground, only returning to the surface due to injury or old age.

As the path curves gently round to the right pause for a moment and look behind you.

This was the site of a serious railway accident which occurred not long after the railway was built. At the time it was common procedure, almost a matter of pride, to load as many wagons behind a locomotive as possible. There was an instance when a train of 99 wagons was assembled north of here at Cinderford and the goods yard was vainly searched for one more. Unfortunately the guard, to his great disappointment, had to leave with only 'ninety nine on'. A train of a hundred wagons was not unusual and in those early days of railway operation good working practices were often learned the hard way.

One such lesson was learnt at this spot in 1863 when an overloaded train of 70 wagons broke in two just north of here. The front end of the train continued on its way while the rear portion gradually fell behind the rest of the train. The orphaned wagons didn't stop however, the falling gradient here ensuring that they continued their journey at reduced speed. The driver eventually noticed his shortage and brought his train to a standstill. Climbing out of the cab to investigate he was immediately aware of an unmistakable rumble from around the curve!

One can only imagine his horror when the 30 truant wagons came into view immediately piling into the back of his train causing a mountain of wreckage that took 5 days to clear.

In 1959 just north of here at a level crossing a driver lost control of his car. He crashed through the gates and was left stranded across the line. The driver of the approaching goods train couldn't stop in time but was relieved to see the driver calmly abandon his vehicle before pausing and rushing back to lock the car door!

Continue to the end of a short cutting where a display board explains the underlying geology of the area. You will be returning to Ruspidge along this route later.

At the road, turn right onto the B4227 before turning almost immediately left into Lower Road. Follow this road through the village until it turns left. At this point continue straight on along a path which climbs to the left of 'Pear Tree Cottage' to reach the track bed of the former Forest of Dean railway.

Soudley

Over to the left is the White Horse pub. This railway was a very steeply graded line and it wasn't unusual to find an engine stopped on the line having literally run out of steam. Strangely enough, this point, next to the White Horse pub, was the point where this was most likely to happen!

Follow the path alongside a car park and when the road drops down keep left along a path on an embankment. Turn left when you re-join the road and look right at a detached garage on an embankment.

This was the site of a level crossing, the railway passing between the garage and the detached gable ended 'Crossing Keeper's Cottage' on the right before disappearing into a tunnel under Bradley Hill. You would have leant on the gate here for a full minute and a half while our 100 wagon train rumbled past completely occupying your field of view.

Your route is immediately to the left of the garage near a way-mark post, where you follow a path which falls into a wooded glade. Like an errant puppy the brook appears again on your right and you cross it using an old packhorse bridge, ignoring a path off left. Follow the path round the foot of the hill keeping the fence on your left.

Below you through some towering beech trees can be seen the Forest of Dean Heritage Centre, which was originally constructed as a corn mill in 1876 being powered by two water-wheels in tandem. The site was subsequently used as a leatherboard mill, a sawmill, a piggery and a car breakers yard and was in near derelict condition when, in 1981, it was bought, restored and converted for use as a museum. The mill is a grade II listed building.

Turn left at the road and after crossing the brook again turn right onto a metalled lane, which passes to the right of some pretty stone cottages.

The wisps of smoke rising from their chimneys and the cackle of hens in their gardens provide an almost timeless charm. Pause just beyond the last one, aptly named Furnace Crossing. To your left can be seem the western portal of the now disused Haie Tunnel which has the distinction of being the world's first railway tunnel, having been built as long ago as 1809 to serve a tramway. A later railway occupied the tunnel in 1854, but being unable to follow the tramways sinuous route past the museum, it required another tunnel which was bored under Bradley Hill to your right about 200m away. Your eye is drawn to its eastern portal by a neat green stretch of lawn. Local people would use Haie tunnel as a short cut to reach Newnham on Severn. It saved many miles of walking but they had to know the railway timetable!

Considering the railway closed as long ago a 1967 it's surprising how much of its route still survives in this overcrowded valley. You get the impression that in an afternoon the tunnels could be re-opened and the track just dropped back into place. Having just left the 1064 yard long Haie tunnel on your left you can just imagine the spluttering engine driver grabbing a quick lungful of air before plunging into Bradley Hill tunnel on your right; although the air would not have been as sweet as it is now because of the heavy industry occupying this valley.

Continue along the path which follows the route of a former tramway which served another foundry further south.

The substantial stone wall on your left is all that remains of two iron works built in 1837, the tramway passing beneath the furnace under a stone arch.

Follow the old tramway around the hillside ignoring a path that climbs steeply past Tump House on your left. Keep the fence to your right and the retaining wall to your left as you round the hillside. The brook returns again until you reach a pretty row of stone cottages. Immediately after the last cottage in the row take a left turn and

Soudley

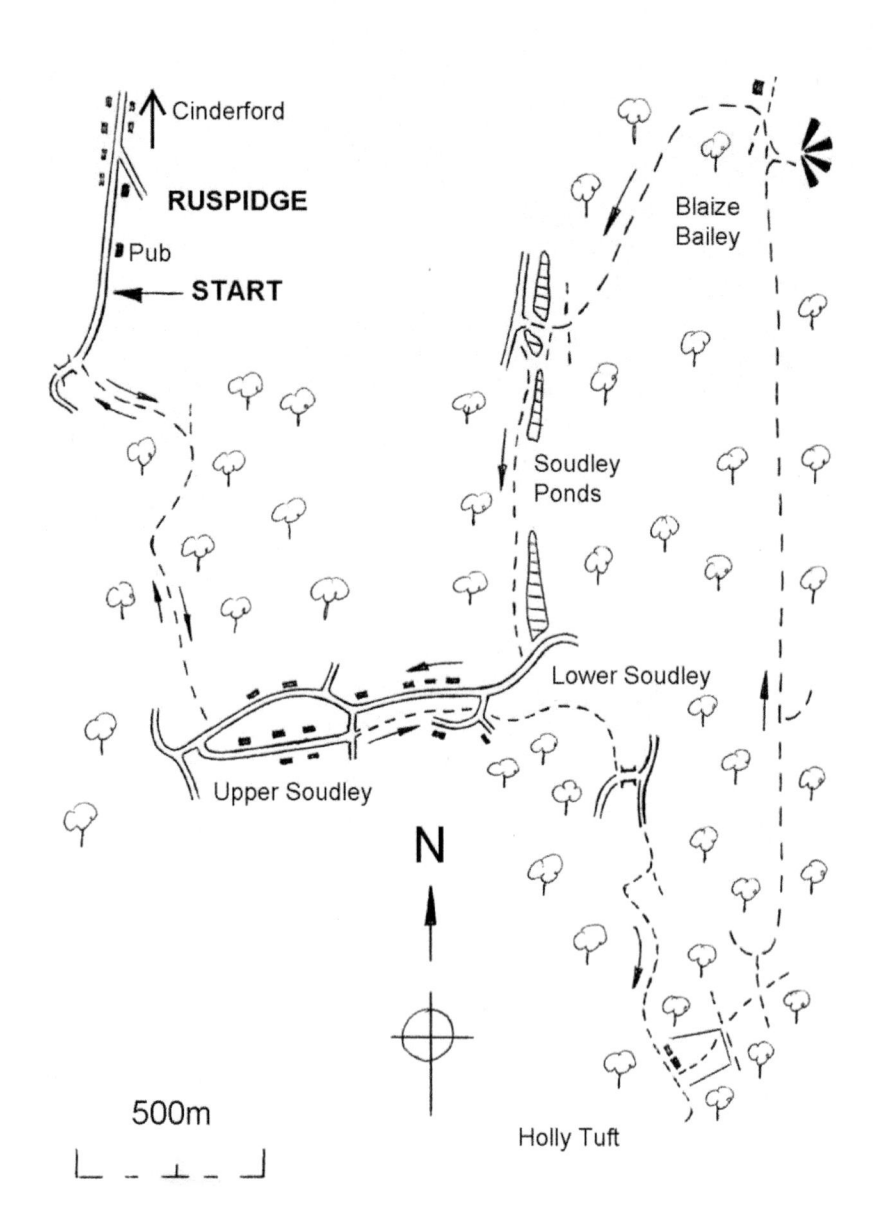

climb up towards a paddock, passing underneath an ornamental bridge. Climb up the steeply rising paddock to reach a gate at the top left corner.

Turn left onto a forest track and, within a few yards, turn right near a yew tree and climb up through the wood on a narrow path. This can be a little overgrown in high summer but with persistence you soon cross another track and, as you crest the hill you turn left onto another track near a yew tree. Soon you reach a bend in a forestry track where you turn right. Walk along this pleasant tree-lined avenue which climbs gently in a northerly direction for well over 1500m until, just where the path begins to descend, a break appears in the trees on your right.

At this point a broad forestry track will take you the short distance to Blaize Bailey viewpoint where a magnificent view is afforded over Newnham, whilst across a great ox-bow bend in the Severn the Cotswold Hills can be seen over 30 km away.

Return to the track which shortly reaches a junction of tracks near a cottage. Follow the obvious route which falls to the left, rapidly losing height as it passes through some tall spruce trees. Eventually the track levels out and reaches another junction.

Ignore tracks on your left and right in favour of one that continues on past a forestry barrier into a car park. Walk between the car park on your left and the pond on your right to reach a road. Turn left here and, within a few metres, take a path on your left which accompanies the road for a short distance before heading into the trees to meet Soudley Ponds.

Soudley

Soudley Ponds

These ponds are a series of five which were constructed in the 1890s for fishing purposes. The ponds at Soudley have been designated a Site of Special Scientific Interest by English Nature because of the dragonflies and beetles that breed here. Dabchicks, moorhens, coots, mandarins and tufted duck all frequent the ponds. The floor of the surrounding woodlands is carpeted with bluebells in spring and foxgloves in early summer. The yellow iris, common in this area, adds a further splash of colour. The spruce trees here reach dizzying heights and there is a real risk of falling over backwards when trying to view them!

When you reach the road turn right, and walk through the village eventually returning to the old railway cutting on the right.

The accompanying display board explains the geology of the route back to Ruspidge, the rock formation at Blue Rock quarry in particular is well worth a visit. This is accessed by a path that climbs steeply to the right under a rocky outcrop just before the disused tunnel.

Retrace your route along the track-bed of the old railway line to the start of the walk.

--------------------<{}>--------------------
God is alive and well, but working on a much less ambitious project

Walk 19: Mallards Pike
Free Miner

A woodland walk which starts at a delightful lakeside picnic area. There are one or two hills and a couple of places where the directions will need to be followed carefully, but you are rewarded with some unusually well preserved industrial archaeology. There is a short exposed section requiring some agility but this should not be beyond the average walker.

Distance	5 miles (8 km)
Route	Mallards Pike – Blackpool Bridge – Stapledge Bungalows
Maps	OS Explorer Map OL14, and OS Landranger 162
Getting there	The walk starts at Mallards Pike which lies on the north side of the B4431 about 3 miles west of Blakeney.
Start/Parking	Mallards Pike Picnic Area which is signposted off the B4431
OS Grid Ref/Postcode	SO637091 / GL15 4HD

Free mining in the Forest of Dean
The free miners owe their rights to their 14th century fore-fathers, who won a battle for King Edward I by tunnelling under castle fortifications at Berwick Upon Tweed. The grateful monarch passed a law which gave local men the right, 'without tax or hindrance', to mine for coal in the Forest of Dean, provided they

Walk in the Wye Valley and Forest of Dean

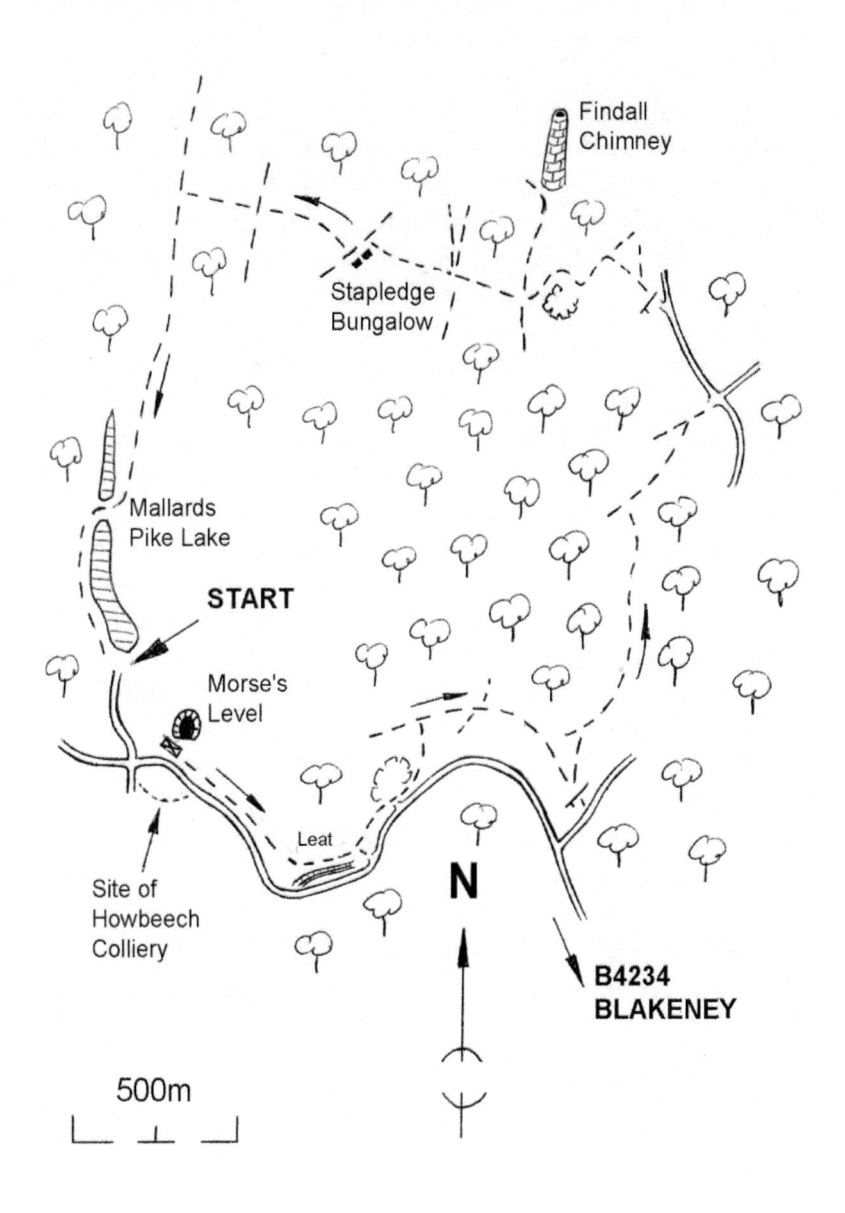

were born within the Forest, were over 21, and had worked down a local coal mine for a year and a day.

Most free miners work alone or with a partner, and their activities are overseen by the Deputy Gaveller from his office in Coleford, where he grants the 'gales', the rights to mine at specific sites. Originally a gale was a tax due to the Crown in recognition of the King's ownership of the land. The Deputy Gaveller still collects the Queen's dues, just as his predecessors did back in the 13th century. Despite the decline of the Forest of Dean coalfield, seventeen free mines were still being worked in 1980 in conditions almost unchanged from their Victorian origins. The men still used picks and shovels to win the coal and worked lying on their stomachs. Nowadays, only a few individuals still work their free mines and even these are worked almost as a hobby. For 700 years the free miners have mined their coal, but now their future is in doubt. The closure of the last maternity hospital within the Forest means that boys will no longer be born within the qualifying area. It is also becoming a problem to persuade new miners to work down the free mines with their antiquated working practices and narrow 2½-3ft coal faces.

The Walk
After parking the car, walk back down the access road which passes over a stone bridge.

This was originally built for the Forest of Dean Central Railway, a freight only line, which was one of the first to reach into the forest from Blakeney in 1856.

Continue down to the road and, after negotiating a cattle-grid, turn left onto the B4431. Cross the road in order to face oncoming traffic and pause for a moment.

The open area to the right was the site of Howbeech Colliery. Traffic along the Central line never lived up to expectations and, for many years, this colliery was the sole source of revenue for the company. Regular traffic ceased with the closure of the colliery in 1921 and the line finally closed in 1942.

Walk along the high grass verge keeping the main road on your left. As the road bends to the right, look to the other side of the road for a gate and adjacent stile on the outside of the bend. Cross the stile and walk round to the right where a few steps lead down to Morse's level, which was opened as long ago as 1826.

Morse's Level

This is a good example of one the few free mines still existing in the Forest. Note the rails leading away from the mine entrance and the stack of pit props used to support the roof which, at the coal face, is less than 750mm from the floor! Morse's Level is mothballed at the time of writing, but such is the transient nature of mining activity that it could be up and running at the time of your visit. Compare this with the working free mine found at the end of the Darkhill walk (walk 14).

Mallards Pike

Return the way you came but instead of walking up to the road turn immediately left and follow a path which runs parallel with the road. This is the former track-bed of the Great Central railway. Eventually you reach a stile after which you drop down right towards the road. The ground is a little uneven here so care should be taken. Between the path and the road is a man-made water channel or 'leat'.

Mining activities in the Forest have always been hampered by the excessive amounts of water encountered underground, the removal of which required a substantial investment in pumping machinery. The underlying stratum here is pervious limestone, and in order to minimise the seepage of water into the mine workings below, the Blackpool Brook is carried over the limestone outcrop in a leat. Subsidence has damaged the leat at some point because most of its water has escaped underground to appear further down the valley as a spring.

Walk alongside the leat for a few metres until a short path off to the right gives access to a road. Ignore this and press on a little further until a quarry appears on the left and another path to the road appears on the right. Go straight on here, climbing steeply round the edge of the quarry. Soon the gradient eases, and after leaving the quarry behind the path rises up to a forestry track. Turn right and follow the obvious route through the woodland for about 800m until a road guarded by a forestry barrier comes into view. Well before the barrier turn left onto a path next to a waymark post. Follow this path up to a 'T' junction where you turn right.

Follow this path for about 500m until it joins a forestry track where you turn right. This track is eventually joined by another, which you follow round to the right, walking past a five-bar gate to reach a road. Turn left here and walk along the road for about 300m until a forestry track appears on the left-hand side. Leave the road here and follow this path up through the woodland for about 400m until another path rises up to meet you on the right. Turn left here, and begin a stiff climb through the trees until the path bends to the right near a couple of hollows.

These are Cudleigh Holes, ancient iron workings, or scowles that date back to Roman times.

Continue up the path, which now bends left, to climb up behind these old workings. As soon as they are out of sight, you arrive at an indistinct crossroads near a bit of wire fence. Your route is straight across, but a right turn here will take you on a short detour to an intact ventilation chimney – possibly the last one remaining in the Forest.

Having turned right, walk along this grassy path between stands of conifers until, after about 300m, it begins a left-hand bend. Look out for some boulders on the outside of the bend and then walk between these into the woodland on the right where, about 40m away, a well preserved brick chimney can be seen.

This 15m chimney was built around 1800 to ventilate the Findall Mine located down in the valley. A fire grate was suspended in the base of the chimney which, when lit, would produce a strong draught effect which sucked stale air from out of the mine. The mine was called Findall because of the variety of minerals that could be found there: 'find all'.

Retrace your steps back to the crossroads you left earlier, and now turn right near the wire fence. Maintain your bearing as you climb up through the woodland until you eventually reach a forestry track. Go straight across here, taking the narrower left-hand path rather than another wider path which leaves the track at an angle. This path can be a little overgrown by ferns in summer but after a little perseverance a white bungalow is glimpsed through the trees on the left. Immediately afterwards, the path reaches a clearing and a forestry track. Turn left here and, as you pass the

Mallards Pike

gateway to a second bungalow, look opposite for a footpath leaving the track on the right. This is your route but pause for a moment and look at the inscription on its gable end.

This is Stapledge Bungalow. Until recent times Oak was of strategic importance, providing shipbuilding material for the Navy. When Lord Nelson visited this area in Napoleonic times he was alarmed by the state of the forest. Uncontrolled felling and grazing had reduced Oak stocks to critical levels. This led to the 'Dean and New Forest Act 1808' which authorised the 'inclosure of land for the production of timber'. Stapledge was the fifth such enclosure in 1809 under the stewardship of Lord Glenbervie Surveyor General of woods. Ordinary Foresters, already poverty stricken, were now denied access to large areas of the forest. This eventually led to riots which were only subdued by infantry from Doncaster and Plymouth. Warren James, leader of the protesters, was transported to Van Diemen's Land (Tasmania) only to be pardoned five years later. He never returned.

Follow your path down the hill, which begins to steepen as you pass through some dense conifers. Cross a forestry track and follow the dusty, cone strewn path down through more conifers, until you emerge at a clearing crossed by a track. Turn left onto this and, accompanied by a power line, follow this for about a kilometre until the track turns right to pass between the two lakes that comprise Mallards Pike. Beyond these turn left, following the lake-side path to the Forestry Commission's log cabin and the car park at the start of the walk.

---------------------<{}>---------------------

Holding a grudge is like drinking poison and expecting the other person to die.

Walk 20: Bradley Hill
Bluebells!

A long gentle climb through some outstanding old woodland to reach a hill with far-reaching views of the Severn Vale. Paths are good throughout.

Distance	4 miles (6.5 km)
Route	Wenchford – Bradley Hill – Blakeney Hill
Maps	OS Explorer Map OL14, and OS Landranger 162
Getting there	The walk starts at the Wenchford Picnic Site near Blakeney
Start/Parking	Park at the Wenchford Picnic Site which is three miles north of Blakeney on the B4431 Parkend Road
OS Grid Ref/Postcode	SO654078 / GL15 4AW

The Walk
Bradley Hill is a magnificent area of deciduous woodland. In autumn, its many paths offer a delightful opportunity to shuffle through the fallen leaves under the shade of its golden canopy. However, the woods are really at their best in early May, when the forest floor is covered by the most spectacular show of bluebells to be seen anywhere.

Walk past the toilet block and information board along a broad track.

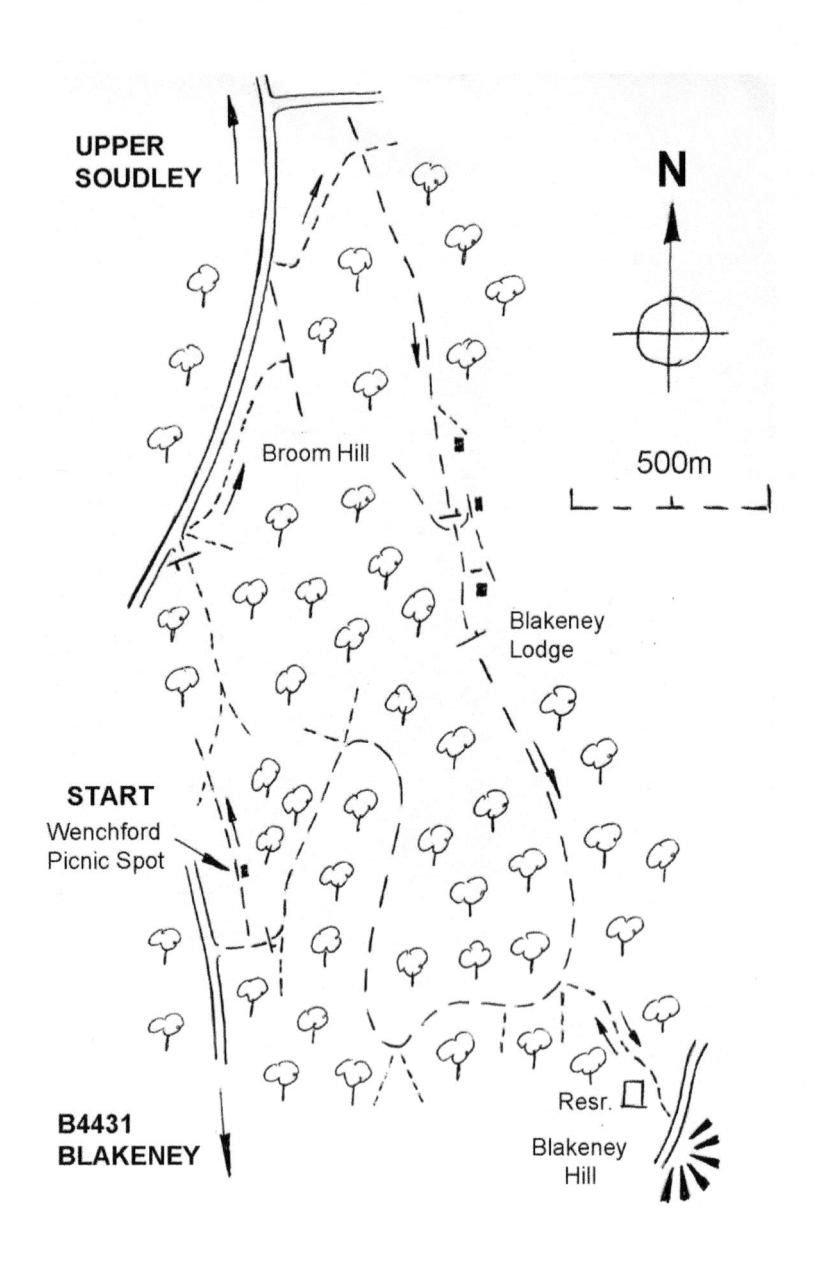

Bradley Hill

UPPER SOUDLEY

Broom Hill

N

500m

Blakeney Lodge

START
Wenchford Picnic Spot

B4431 BLAKENEY

Resr.
Blakeney Hill

This is the track bed of the grandly named Forest of Dean Central Railway, one of the first to reach into the Forest from Blakeney in 1856. This was a freight-only line, being constructed to provide an outlet for forest coal, stone and iron ore. Traffic along the route did not live up to expectations and, by 1869, there was only enough to occupy one engine on alternate days. It closed in 1942.

Down to your left the under the dappled shade of oak trees the Blackpool Brook trickles through the picnic site which is very popular in the summer months.

After a while the path runs parallel to the old track-bed which occupies a cutting on the right, after which you pass between a number of stone blocks. About 50m beyond these leave the track-bed on the right using a path indicated by a way-mark post bearing a white chevron. Follow this path down through the trees and, ignoring a path which joins from the right, continue through the woodland with the railway embankment high up on your left. Eventually, after negotiating a forestry barrier, you reach a road. Ignore the road and take the second of the two paths that leave the road here on the right. Follow this faint path up through the woodland, keeping the stream and road a short distance away on your left. After meandering steeply up to a forest track you turn left and wander down to the road. Here, another path leads away to the right, but ignore this and follow the road for about 50m to find another path which leaves the road on the right. This bends left to climb gently up through the woodland.

If you are walking this route in early May, you will now see waves of bluebells flooding the woodland floor like a rising tide. Wonderfully complemented by the new leaves of the oak and beech, they have waited until the luminous green canopy has almost closed over before rushing up into the sunlight.

For many people this is one of nature's magical sights, an enduring symbol of springtime and the coming to life of the countryside. Please be aware that it is illegal to dig up the bulbs of wild bluebells. Witnessing the sea of blue before you it's hard to believe that they are, in fact, an endangered species!

Bradley Wood

Eventually, where the path levels out, you reach a broad track. Turn right here and follow this broad track as it descends gently through the woodland.

The track soon starts to climb again and, after passing a white painted house it reaches a junction of tracks below a power line. Ignore the track on the left and continue along with the power line for company until, as you bear slightly left, the power line drops downhill away to the right. Pass a forestry barrier and follow a broad track through the conifers for about a kilometre until you reach a junction of paths.

You turn left here to take a short path to Blakeney Hill, but will be returning to this spot later, when your eventual route will follow the broad track which descends to the right.

Follow the path off to the left where shortly it emerges onto a narrow lane near a reservoir. Turn right, and walk a few paces down the lane for a sweeping view of the Severn Vale.

Out of sight below you, astride the A48, is the village of Blakeney, while in the distance Berkeley Nuclear Power station can be seen. Built in 1962, its twin reactors were sited on the estuary because of the availability of large amounts of cooling water. It was capable of generating enough electricity to serve an urban area the size of Bristol, but was de-commissioned in 1989.

Retrace your steps back to the right-hand side of the reservoir, being careful to pick the correct path back into the woodland. Follow the path back through the trees and, after returning to the spot mentioned earlier, follow the forestry track down the hill taking the obvious route as it meanders through the woodland. A couple of paths head off to the left as the track swings right, but ignore these and continue on down the hill. Soon a power line accompanies you for a while before climbing away to the right. Shortly afterwards the track bends left at a junction of paths. Descend through the woods until the track swings left then right to teach a forestry barrier. Round the barrier and turn right to reach the picnic site and the start of the walk.

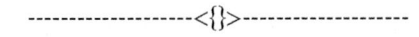

--------------------<{}>--------------------

Blowing out the other person's candle will not make yours shine brighter

Walk 21: Flaxley
Saints and sinners!

This walk, which has a spiritual theme, passes through quiet woodland and pretty valleys to visit a number of sites of historic interest. One or two paths may be muddy especially after rain. Careful navigation will be needed in places but since when has the path to redemption been easy?

Distance	4½ miles (7 km)
Route	Littledean – Flaxley – Green Bottom
Maps	OS Explorer Map OL14, and OS Landranger 162
Getting there	The walk starts near Littledean Jail which is just outside Littledean on the A4151.
Start/Parking	Park in a small lay-by just south of Littledean Jail on the opposite side of the road
OS Grid Ref/Postcode	SO673136 / GL14 3NL

The walk
Cross the road and walk down the hill past Littledean Jail.

When this remarkable Grade II listed building was built in 1791, it was seen as the most modern house of correction of its time, many of its innovative design features being used in the construction of London's Pentonville Prison. The first inmate was Joseph Marshall,

Walk in the Wye Valley and Forest of Dean

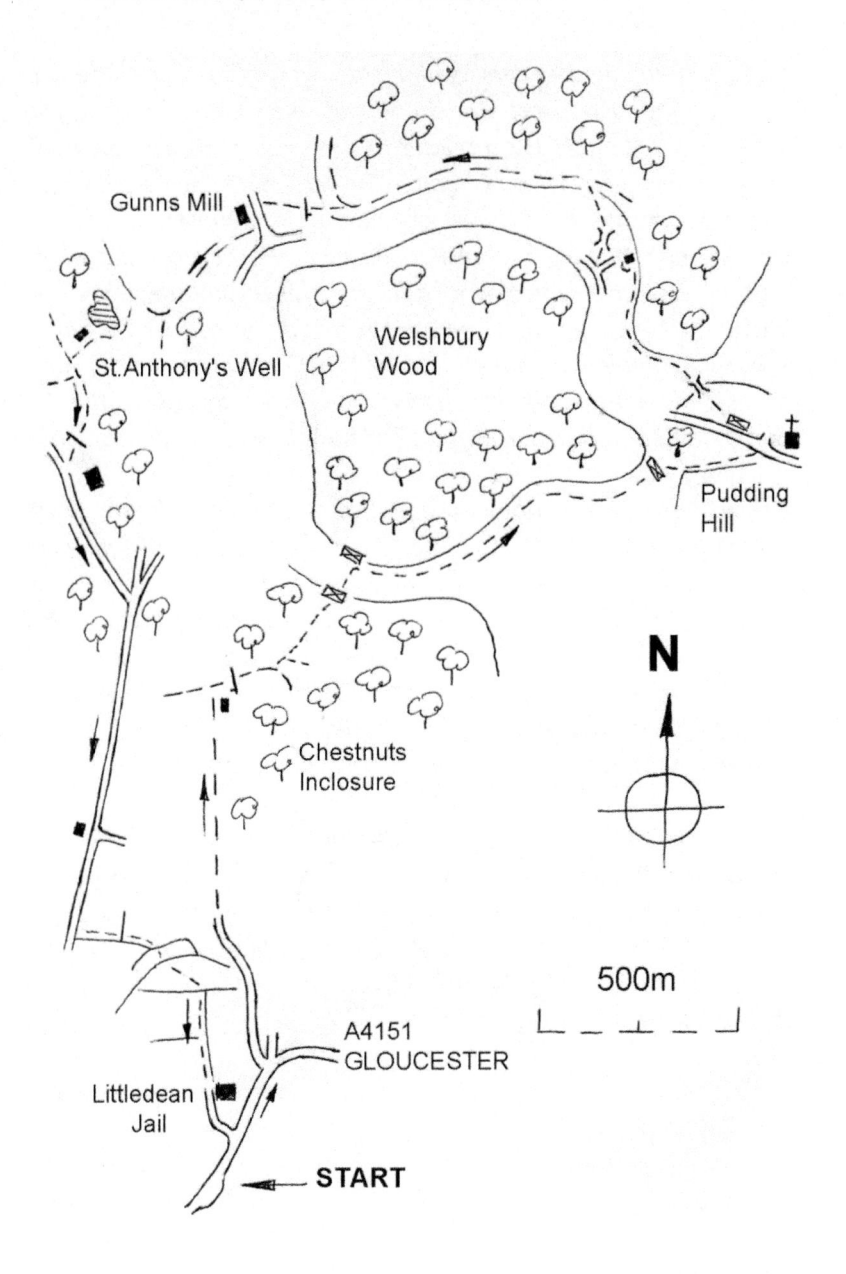

Flaxley

a 19 year old labourer convicted of stealing a spade, but there was no segregation and records show that even in the brief period between 1837 and 1838 three births were recorded with only one of the infants surviving. Female prisoners were incarcerated for lewdness or petty theft, whilst their male counterparts might typically be interned for desertion, fraud, embezzlement, assault or murder. Child convicts as young as eight were punished by being birched or whipped, and sometimes found themselves placed in solitary confinement. Not surprisingly, having witnessed so much misery, the jail has gained a reputation for being haunted and a number of paranormal investigations have been carried out.

Behind the austere gatehouse entrance and its 5 metre high sandstone walls, the prison remains almost unchanged from when it was first built. Steeped in history and infamy, its awesome appearance is a stark reminder of the hard labour and craftsmanship needed to build this architecturally important jailhouse. The last prisoner left in 1854, after which it was used as a police station and courthouse until the 1980s when an insurance company used it to site their mainframe computer and archives.

It is now open as a tourist attraction housing an extensive collection of crime memorabilia collected over 25 years by its owner who lives on the premises. While some of the jail has been converted to family accommodation, almost all of the cells remain, together with the former courtroom and treadmill. Needless to say it is well worth a visit.

Walk past the jail and, after about 200m, turn onto 'Greenway', the first of two lanes that leave the road as it bends to the right. Eventually the tarmac gives way to an old farm track that climbs gently uphill between a paddock and some old woodland. After about 500m you reach the top of the climb at a junction of paths just beyond a cottage on the right. Turn right here, passing through a forestry barrier to follow a track through stands of oak and beech. As the track bends right, turn left, following the track until it drops down to a gate. Opposite you, across a narrow strip of pasture, another gate and stile beckon, but after walking across to them, they must be ignored in favour of an indistinct path that bears right, to follow the edge of the woodland downhill.

Keep the boundary of the woodland on your left, and avoid the temptation to drop to the right. Shortly views open up across the valley to the right while in the distance the Severn shimmers in the sunlight. Keeping the valley on your right, you cling to the edge of the woodland for the next 700m, passing through a succession of stiles and gates. After passing through a final gate you emerge onto an open area which drops steeply away on both sides. Walk to the right of the oak tree in front of you to reach a fence a few metres beyond, where you turn left. Walk down the hill with the fence on your right until you pass a yew tree, where you can pause for a moment to enjoy the view across the valley.

This is the scattered village of Flaxley, now a picturesque rural backwater but once a busy industrial area with furnaces, forges and mills. The earliest known forge dates back to 1150 and at least five mills have been identified as utilising the waters of Westbury Brook, which runs across the valley in front of you. Flaxley is also famous for its old Cistercian abbey founded between 1148 and 1154 by Roger, Earl of Hereford, at the spot where his father, Miles of Gloucester, was killed whilst out hunting. The abbey and its monks were granted considerable rights over the surrounding woodland, which the Brothers put to good use, firing forges to smelt the local iron ore. The abbey prospered until the Dissolution in 1536-7 when its lands and manor were granted to Sir William Kingston, the Constable of the Tower of London (who supervised the execution of Ann Boleyn). In 1648 the abbey and all its possessions were sold to William and James Boeve (later Boevey) who were members of London's Dutch community, the estate remaining in the family until well into the 20th century. Across the valley, the substantial 18th century house incorporates the remains of the monastery and perpetuates the name of the Abbey.

Aiming for the church, drop steeply down to the corner of the field where you cross a stile to reach a minor road.

This is St. Mary's, Flaxley, originally a gateway chapel of the Abbey which became a church following the dissolution, when the abbey became a mansion. The church was rebuilt in 1856 using contrasting red and grey forest stone, and has a richly decorated interior containing many of the features found in the earlier chapel including many Boevey family memorials.

Turn left at the road, and after about 30m look right for a pair of wooden gates. Pass through these and bear left, heading for a gap in the left hand boundary of the field. This boundary is actually the course of the Westbury Brook and, after crossing it, bear left to follow the edge of the woodland around the valley. Shortly you arrive at a cottage bounded by a hedgerow, where you turn left to follow a track up to a country lane. Don't walk onto the lane; instead look over your right shoulder to find a path that heads off at an angle, passing across the stream to reach the boundary of the woodland. Here, cross a stile and follow the path through the trees to a forestry track, at which you turn left. Follow this round the edge of the valley until the track swings right. Go straight ahead here and walk past a forestry barrier to eventually reach a minor road. Turn left here and, on reaching the road junction, turn right into Lower Spout Lane, a rough track which climbs steeply past Guns Mill, now the subject of a restoration project.

This was originally a blast furnace belching sulphurous smoke across the valley. Built by Sir John Wintour, and operated between 1629 and 1743, it was named after William Gunne, the owner of an earlier mill on the site. Guns Mill was used primarily for armament production and, in 1629, over 600 guns were ordered by the Crown for use in Holland, but many were subsequently used by both sides in the English Civil War. The furnace was destroyed by order of Parliament in 1650, but was rebuilt in 1683 and remained in use until 1743 when it became a paper mill. The latter closed in 1879 but several of the furnace buildings remain, and the site is now a scheduled monument being the country's finest remaining example of a charcoal blast furnace from this period.

Follow the track uphill into the woodland, where it eventually makes a sweeping right turn. Ignore a path to the left that heads invitingly up into the woods, and continue on round the bend until a pond is spotted on the left, shaded by oak and beech. Turn left here and, keeping to the left of the pond, climb up the obvious dip in the hillside to reach St Anthony's Well, an ancient spring whose name dates from the medieval period.

St Anthony's Well

Its waters are said to cure skin complaints but, to get the full benefit, you need to make nine visits in the month of May. In Victorian times the well was used by a local Baptist minister for christenings. If, after comparing the forbidding jail with the beautiful Abbey, you've reached any spiritual conclusions then now is your chance, but be assured, the water is always cold!

Flaxley

Climb steeply up behind the well to reach a path where you turn left. The path now winds through oak and beech until eventually, accompanied by a power line, it climbs steeply up to a forestry track where you turn left. This track passes to the right of the Green Bottom Water Works which supplies fresh water to the district by pumping it up from subterranean mine-workings. After passing the works, turn left onto a metalled track which leads eventually to a minor road. Turn right here and, after about 500m, look for 'Greenway', an unsurfaced lane which appears on the left opposite a cottage named 'Pike House'. Ignore this and continue straight on for another 250m to find a footpath leaving the road on the left. Follow this path alongside a paddock, keeping the fence on your right, until you drop down to a stile. Cross a short strip of land beyond this to find a stile in a hedgerow. Climb up the next field, looking for a gate 50m to the right of a tree. Pass through this gate and, keeping the next field boundary on your left, crest the hill after which the jail comes into view. Follow the path keeping the jail on your left until you reach the road.

Also in the area, but unconnected with this walk is an old gold mine. It is located at grid ref 644195. But before you rush off to stake a claim, the gold was not found in sufficient quantity to justify the expense involved, and the mine closed early in the 20th Century. The mine was mentioned in walk 17 but only now, having progressed to walk 21, is its true location revealed!

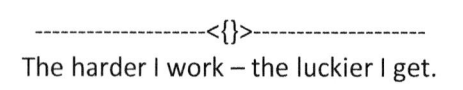

--------------------<{}>--------------------
The harder I work – the luckier I get.

Walk 22: Newent Daffodils
Enjoy a Wordsworth moment!

The daffodils that captivated Wordsworth were seen by him in his native Lake District, but you too can experience, in large numbers, the flowers that inspired his classic verse. The route follows the course of an old canal before returning though some outstanding woodland, and is best walked in early spring when the daffodils are at their best and the cold dark winter is easing its grip. The route is mainly level with one or two easy gradients; paths are generally good, but there are a few muddy spots.

Distance	7½ miles (12 km)
Route	Newent – Oxenhall Tunnel – Betty Daws Wood – Hay Wood
Maps	OS Explorer Map OL14
Getting there	The walk starts in Newent. Leave Newent on the B4221 Ross road then turn right into Horsefair Lane (signposted Oxenhall and Kempley). Within about 100m, the lane broadens out in front of a bungalow on the left and a timber yard on the right.
Start/Parking	There is ample parking in front of the bungalow, or in the wide entrance to the timber yard, but be careful not to block access to either
OS Grid Ref/Postcode	SO717263 / GL18 1RP

The walk

Walk along the lane away from Newent for about 400m until on your right you reach Horsefair Wharf – the workshops of the Hereford to Gloucester Canal Trust.

The H & G Canal Trust is a volunteer organisation that has, since 1983, been working to restore the canal with the ultimate aim of reinstating the route between Hereford and Gloucester.

Take a footpath to your right, just before the wharf, and follow it round to the back of the trust's premises and then bear left to cross an aqueduct.

This was the route of both the Hereford to Gloucester canal and the similarly named railway, which was built over the old canal at this point.

Construction of the canal started at Gloucester in 1793 at the height of 'canal mania' and reached Ledbury in 1798. However, the cost of construction had been so great and the resulting revenues so small, that no further progress was made for 50 years. After this long pause the canal company resumed construction, reaching Hereford without ceremony in 1845. This was almost the age of 'railway mania' and within a few years the Worcester-Hereford railway opened, complete with a station at Ledbury. The over-spend on the northern extension of the canal to Hereford had been so great, that the canal company manager travelled to Birmingham intending to borrow more money. He returned empty-handed using the newly opened railway, remarking on its great comfort and reliability! This was an echo of the many anti- Beeching protest meetings arranged a century later that were attended by car.

The canal was unable to compete and, in 1863, it was leased to the railway company who eventually built a railway over parts of

Walk in the Wye Valley and Forest of Dean

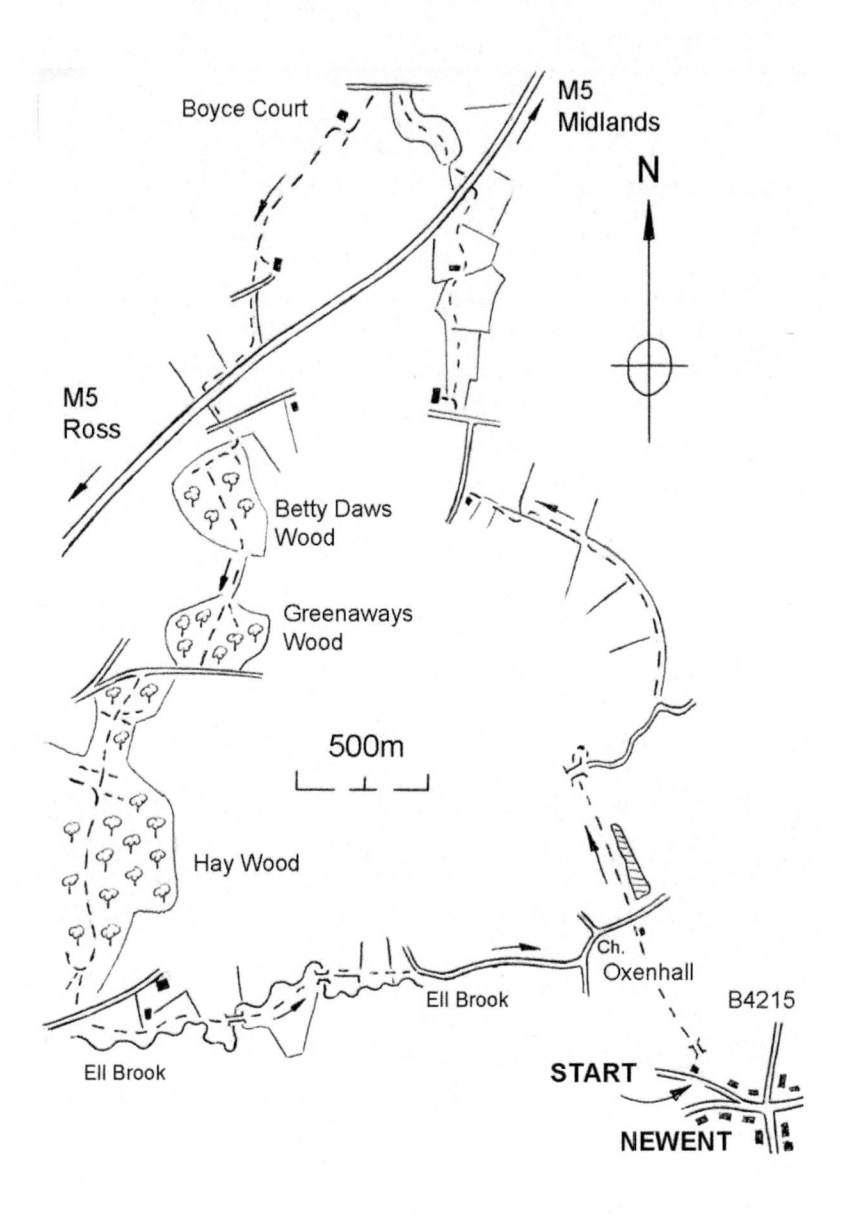

the canal route, which finally reached Gloucester in 1885. The northern section of the canal between Ledbury and Hereford remained, but without the rest of the route to Gloucester together with its isolation from the rest of the canal network, it gradually drifted into obscurity.

Follow the towpath along the old canal which emerges from underneath the railway track-bed, now seen as a low embankment on your left.

You shortly reach Oxenhall lock, restored by the trust in the late 1990s and now privately owned.

Continue past the cottage until you reach a road. Look left here at lonely Oxenhall church – you will be returning this way later.

Pick up the tow path on the other side of the road and follow it to the brick ellipse of Coldharbour Bridge.

The water on the right was originally a storage pond built to serve a blast furnace at nearby Newent. This is a popular spot for herons, which rise lazily from the pond with a few flaps of their wings.

Your route leaves the old canal immediately after the bridge by climbing right for a few paces to reach a lane but, if time allows, walk on for a few hundred metres to the southern portal of Oxenhall tunnel (this may not be possible in high summer when the towpath becomes quite overgrown).

Over 1500m long, this tunnel was the most difficult part of the route and was instrumental in the destiny of the canal. Water ingress during construction was so great that it could only be kept dry by using a number of steam pumping engines. This exhausted the canals' funds and was the main reason for the delay in the completion of the route to Hereford.

Return to the bridge and take what is now a left turn onto a country lane. After a gentle climb of a few hundred metres, the lane bends to the right. Look for a path that leaves the lane on the left near a power line. Turn right on entering the field, and keep to the left of the hedgerow for the next three fields. Cross a stream at the bottom of the third field where another storage pond can be seen to the right. Climb up through an orchard keeping its well-managed apple trees on your right. Go through a kissing gate at the top of the field and turn right, keeping to the left of a hedgerow for two fields. As the boundary of the second field curves to the left, pass through a gate on the right after which you turn left. The route is not obvious here, but the path passes close to the right hand side of a cottage, before reaching a country lane at which you turn right.

Walk along the lane and eventually turn left at a T-junction. After a few hundred metres, turn right near a power line onto a track leading to Castlemoor Farm. As the track swings to the left, continue straight on over a stile and look for another on the other side of the field, neatly framed in the supports of a power line. Cross this second stile and walk down the left hand side of a large field.

If you have chosen the right time of year you will experience your first 'Wordsworth' moment as, just beyond two old oak trees, 'fluttering and dancing in the breeze' is a field littered with daffodils!

Continue towards a stile in the far corner, ignoring two gates in the field's left-hand boundary. Go over this stile, and after passing to the right of an oak tree, cross another just to the right of some old farm buildings. Walk down this field, aiming to the left of a pond in its far corner, and cross a further stile. Road noise from the nearby M50 becomes more noticeable and, half-way down the left-hand side of this field, turn left to reach the other side of it using a subway.

The M50 has an interesting history by motorway standards. It was one of the first to be constructed, leaving the A38 north of Tewkesbury in 1958 and heading south west, with lofty ambitions of being part of a strategic route between the Midlands and the Welsh coal fields. By the time it was built, the country was leaving behind the economic restrictions of the 1950s and could afford to plan, and then build, a better route across the Severn. The motorway is now regarded as one of most scenic in the country; the section through Dymock Woods is particularly colourful in spring when daffodil crowd the road side. When the motorway was first opened, motorists were unfamiliar with the restrictions on its use and some stopped to pick the flowers – one party even set up a picnic table in the central reservation! The road has hardly changed since it was built and its junctions have not been upgraded to modern standards. Its entry and exit points are hardly any more than breaks in the motorways boundary fence! A truly unique piece of motorway which starts in rural Gloucestershire, and finishes in rural Herefordshire.

On the other side of the motorway, cross the field and head for a copse half way up the left-hand side. Just beyond a farm gate look for a way-mark post next to a stile, and walk into the copse.

Another Wordsworth moment awaits you inside where hundreds of daffodil can be seen in a glance 'tossing their heads in sprightly dance'.

Follow the path through this beautiful copse passing over two footbridges. To your left is the enormous cutting leading away from the northern end of Oxenhall Tunnel, excavated by an army of navvies armed with nothing more sophisticated than a pick and shovel.

"Dancing and fluttering in the breeze"

Eventually, a large brick-built canal bridge comes into view. Turn left onto the bridge and, just beyond it, turn left again, passing between two stone gate-posts to walk into Boyce Court. At the end of the drive don't go straight on but dog leg right past a landscaped pond before crossing a cattle grid. Your route is now a farm track which heads off towards some distant farm buildings. Eventually the track bends to the left to reach them, but you go straight on, walking through an open five-bar gate in a high hedgerow to reach the field beyond. Keep to the left of this field and cross the farm's access road using two kissing gates. Head up the left side of the next field, reaching a brook that spreads out into a tree lined pond. Ahead of you the M50 obstructs the route, so at the top of the field turn right, following the motorway embankment into a second field where you turn left into a large subway. If you listen carefully here the Talking Heads' song, *We're*

Newent Daffodils

on the Road to Nowhere, can be heard above the relentless roar of tyres on tarmac.

Follow the path beyond the motorway, heading for gate in the right hand corner of this narrow field.

The former Hereford to Gloucester railway line followed the left hand boundary of this field; the low brick wall at the far end being the top of a bridge which carried a road over a cutting, now filled in. Like many rural lines, traffic declined with the arrival of road transport and, in 1959, the Ledbury-Dymock section closed to passengers. The Gloucester end continued to be used for goods traffic until Dr Beeching caught up with it in 1964.

Cross the road and take a path beyond a five-bar gate, which heads across a small field to a stile at the corner of a wood. Go through the stile and immediately look for an old farm gate on the right which takes you into the wood. Once inside, ignore a path that goes left in favour of another that goes straight ahead. In about 150m turn left, to follow a path which gently descends in a south-south-easterly direction.

This is Betty Daws Wood; a superb example of an ancient sessile oak wood. The sessile is one of our two native oaks and favours rather acidic soil, usually found on the poorer hill soils of north and west Britain. As well as oaks, Betty Daws wood also contains wild cherry, ash, some wild service tree, and small-leaved lime – these last two are indicators of ancient woodland. The reserve is best known for its spectacular show of wild daffodil, accompanied by wood anemone, bluebell, and primrose. Here you gaze across another golden display and again the great bard comes to mind: 'I gazed and gazed but little thought, what wealth the show to me had brought'. They have recently flourished thanks to coppicing of the hazel and path-widening, which has allowed sunlight to filter down to the woodland floor. The wood has a good bird count including pied and spotted flycatcher, nuthatch, wren, treecreeper, marsh tit, dunnock, song thrush, and garden warbler. You also have a good chance of seeing many woodland butterflies, notably white admiral, wood-white, and silver-washed fritillary.

Immediately after crossing another path, exit through a gate at the bottom of the wood and, ignoring another gate on the left, walk down the left hand side of a field. Cross the bridge at the bottom and enter Greenaways wood.

Bear slightly right and take the more obvious of the two paths that head into the wood, reaching a road on the far side beyond a barrier, where a small nature reserve occupies a narrow strip of land alongside the road.

This is Gwen and Vera's Fields, which represent two of the few remaining daffodil meadows once typical of the area. Pause by the information board for the best view of the riot of wild flowers.

Turn right onto the road and walk for about 250m until, opposite a pretty roadside cottage, you leave the road on the left to pass through a forestry barrier into Shaw Common.

Here the daffodils perform once more: 'And then my heart with pleasure fills, and dances with the daffodils'. They do not have things all their own way here, but have to compete for your attention with large carpets of wood anemones, who almost deserve a verse of their own.

Walk straight ahead into the wood, eventually crossing two closely spaced stiles, to follow the path which heads in a south-south-east direction into Hay Wood. Soon after crossing another path, you make a junction with a bend in a broad track. Go straight on here, following the track for some distance until, after dropping down to cross a brook, the track climbs up again to eventually turn sharp right, almost doubling up on itself. Leave the track here, taking the furthest left of two paths which leave the outside of the bend.

Follow this path through the woodland until you arrive at a lane. Look for a farm gate on the other side, and take the path beyond which follows a brook on the right hand side of the field.

This area was once a small coalfield but most of the old workings have disappeared into the landscape. When the canal was being built, great play was made of the potential of this coalfield, and the canal company constructed a branch which reached out from Newent so its output could be taken economically to market. Ironically, the quality of the coal mined here was so poor that the building of the canal simply enabled better coal to be imported from outside the area.

At the end of the field, cross a farm gate to the right of a barn. Follow a power line round to the right, heading for a stile in the far left corner of the field under the third pole. Climb up to the stile and turn right, following the field round to the next pole. Walk beyond this for about 100m until a footbridge carries you across the Ell Brook. Head for a distant power pole which you pass on the left. Ignore an inviting footbridge here and press on into the corner of the field keeping the hedgerow on your left. Cross a footbridge here and immediately look to the left for a farm gate. Pass through this and turn right, keeping to the left of a fence until you reach a gate in the corner. Keep to the right of the next field to reach a gate in the right corner, ignoring a metal bridge that invites you over the brook. Pass through this gate and walk towards another at the end of a small field. Beyond this turn right onto a lane, which soon crosses the old railway before reaching a junction with another lane. Bear left here, signposted Kempley, and after a short climb turn right at Oxenhall Church. Follow the lane downhill for about 100m until you pass a private drive on the right.

Note the water course which runs alongside it. This is all that remains of the canal branch which left the main route here to reach the coal-field mentioned earlier.

Turn right just beyond the private drive and return to the start of the walk passing Oxenhall Lock cottage en-route.

--------------------<{}>--------------------

The difference between a clown and a middle aged man is that the clown knows he's wearing silly clothes

Bibliography

Bibliograpy

The Archaeology and History of Ancient Dean and the Wye Valley.
Cyril Hart. Thornhill Press, 1992

A Child of the Forest.
Winifred Foley. Futura Publications, 1977

A History of Railways in the Forest of Dean Part 1 – The Great Western
HW Parr. David and Charles, 1971

A History of Railways in the Forest of Dean Part 2 – The Severn and Wye
HW Parr. David and Charles, 1973

An Illustrated History of the Severn and Wye Railway.
Pope, How & Karue. Berkshire Wild Swan Publications, 1985

The Industrial History of the Forest of Dean.
Dr Cyril Hart. David and Charles, 1971

Man of iron – man of steel; the lives of David and Robert Mushet.
Ralph Anstis. Albion House, 1997

The Mines of the Forest of Dean and Surrounding areas.
Tony Oldham. Anne Oldham, 2002

The Mines of Newent and Ross.
David Bick. Hyperion Books, 1987

The Old Industries of Dean.
David Bick. Pound House, 1980

The River Wye.
Keith Kissack. Terence Dalton, 1985

Ross and Monmouth Railway.
Mark Glover. Brewin Books, 1994

The Story of Parkend.
Ralph Anstis. Lightmoor Press, 2009

The Story of the Mushets.
FM Osborn. Thomas Nelson and Sons, 1952

The Wye Valley.
Sale and Waite. Hounslow, Wildwood House, 1984

The Wye Valley Railway and Coleford Branch.
Handley & Dingwall. Oakwood Press, 1998

Bibliography

Other books by this author:

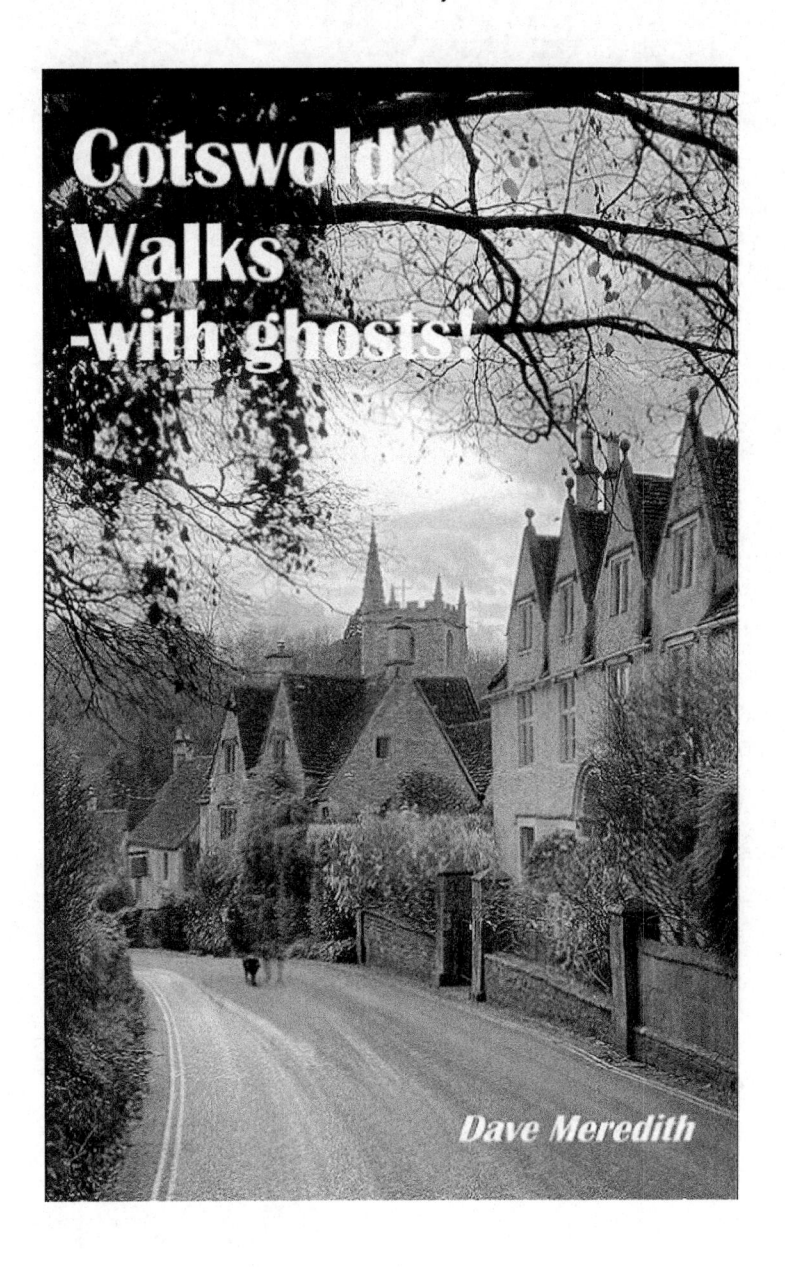

Cotswold Walks -with ghosts!

Dave Meredith

Bibliography

Cotswold Walks
-with children!

Dave Meredith

PROSTATE CANCER
A race between two snails

David Meredith

Printed in Great Britain
by Amazon